It's Time to Wake

... . Lightfoot

IT'S TIME TO WAKE UP THE TREES

First edition. March 21, 2023.

Copyright © 2023 Andromeda Lightfoot.

ISBN: 979-8215204511

Written by Andromeda Lightfoot.

It's Time to Wake up the Trees

Andromeda Lightfoot

Published by Andromeda Light Press, 2023.

For my beautiful Daughter. May you always stand in your truth, may your heart always know you are loved, may your mind and spirit always be free to travel the innerverse and meet your God, face to face. I love you.

Acknowledgements:

Firstly, to the infinite Creator of all things, Divine Spirit of the innerverse, the all that is, this is my love-song to 'you.' I give thanks for this life and all moments that have brought me to this point of awareness, right now. I am grateful for each expression of God in my life. For every challenge, every act of kindness given, for every sacrifice and moment of reconciliation, I am grateful.

Special thanks go to Jo and Tonya Cannariato who have been so generous with their time, encouragement, talent and patience. Tonya, thank you for being such a great editor and force for good in all of our lives and Jo, you're my bro in spirit, music and sound.

To my friend and spiritual bro Vinny M Grant (vinnymgrant.com), thank you for your incredible ground-breaking change-work which helped me to expand this consciousness enough to go far beyond my 'self', through the inner dimensions and into the 'I am that I am.' The best is yet to come.

Professional: Professor Andrew Hague, Professor Alan Rice, Bill Donahue and all the awakened trees who have shared their knowledge and wisdom along the way.

Personal: Thank you to Fergus and all the family, Steve Lecaz, :Conrad Born, Tracy and Tony Symons, Michelle Stevens, Trev, :dean and all at empowerthepeople.com, :Vanessa, Sylvia, Debbie Hartley, Lynnie, Hilary Jacques,Kay and all at TLN, Karen Hamlin, Sarah Hayes, Andrew Peacock, Christopher David - may all your days be golden, Cliff, Will in Africa, Craig

Whitewood-Khan and all those who have been surrogate sons and daughters over the years.

For links, images and references, please go to the end notes.

Prelude

———

"It's time to wake up the Trees"As I sat among the roots of an old, gnarled tree who had called me into the glade, I wept... I wept because I had not spoken to a tree since I was seventeen. Although my connection was still there, always admiring them, perhaps I had forgotten their meaning, neglecting the acknowledgement of the Earth on which we both lived? Instead, I opted for prayers and worship in the opposite direction. Always aiming for the sky and the divine masculine, the father God of the skies, ignoring the divinely feminine Earth beneath my feet. It's been a long journey of awakening, but my time to speak is now. My story will give a context to the insights I have expressed here but should be read generically in relation to how this might serve you in your journey.

I'm not alone. My ability to join the dots together is somewhat of a movement right now, but there are pieces missing. The knowledge is fragmented, and I've been waiting for the right time to fill in some gaps. In this book, I seek to show how the truth is hiding in plain sight. I seek to demystify symbols, myths, and legends to show us who we really are. We've been lied to, indoctrinated, and made to feel unworthy, which in itself causes mass psychosis. But the truth is written in our hearts and minds and nothing, no nothing, can separate us from that forever. The truth will out.

At this time, it's important that we discern the difference between truth and falsehood so that we might heal each others' wounds and "walk each other home." Black, white, Asian, and all people, everywhere, need to heal. In this book, I will show you some things that might inspire you think differently, change your perception, rekindle a memory, and perhaps might validate all you've been feeling consciously and unconsciously as you've journeyed through this timeline.

During this time of global awakening, people are making decisions out of fear. I trust that the contents of this book might remove that fear and that as we transition into our best selves, the process will be made easier through some of the information here.

And so, I'll begin. In 2018, I heard an inner voice say: "Research the pineal gland."

As a born-again Christian, this was not allowed, and was, in fact, considered the enemy's camp. As a seer and someone who had grown up in an occult background, I knew there was nothing to fear. I'd studied the Bible intensely for seven years, had a deliverance ministry, had been a worship leader, and was delivered myself from freemasonry and other unwanted extras left over from my occult-oriented childhood, so I dived in.

As I began writing this book, I had no idea just how incredibly obfuscated the Bible (and other scripts) actually were and how difficult it would be to make any sense out of what was hiding in front of me. The pages had been seriously messed with and contaminated, politically repurposed and edited, and it's only now that I really comprehend the reason.

Most of the stories and sacred knowledge have been stolen from Ancient Afro-Egyptian texts. These have been all but destroyed and fragmented along with their authors, who were, as a result, enslaved and suppressed for thousands of years.

Reset after reset, time after time, the indoctrination of our ancestors, who were just children, resulted in programming and ignorance of who we are and where we came from. The abolition of our true history and its culturally narcissistic replacement has caused a never-ending battle between good and cultured, invented evil.

Remember, we are told that most people didn't write, which means that those who did could say anything they wanted to, and people would agree. Personally, I think history is littered with lies; when you look objectively at books like the Bible, you can see that it was not written six-thousand years ago. Critical thinking will tell you that.

And so, as I went deeper into researching and writing the forthcoming pages, I realised I had to let go of all I had relied upon to give me stability. It's been a trip, and I have fallen more than a few times. I have reached up and dug down only to find that the truth is written in my DNA, and that as I tune into my inner harp, my inner constellations ignite and start to play divine music. My love-song to God.

And, when everything else in the world looks like it's crumbling, I remember the majesty of the tree, how the roots dig deep into the Earth and create the wood wide web. The unseen communication between every tree on the planet. The grid of mycelium that allows us to breathe.

I think of the birds sitting in each branch, singing the stomata open at dawn. We are like trees. We are the tree of life. Our energy grid lights up and its fruit, the pineal, like mycelium, communicates with our creator. We are awakening en masse. From our toes to the Arbor Vitae, Cerebellum to Ammon's Horn, our consciousness is expanding and joining as one with the universal, multi-versal love frequencies and infinite dimensions.

It's time to wake up the trees.

Chapter One: Introduction

———

In this book, you *may* learn about who and what you really are. You may de-mystify the "scripts" that have been playing out as non-allegorical, theatrical dramas, through the "church" and other factions, misleading the masses into false beliefs and disempowering, fruitless searches for truth. You could inner-stand (from here forward, I will use this coinage as innerstand to reflect the inward nature of the understanding I am promoting) the incredible creation that you are. All that was confusing to you may become clear, if you have eyes to see and ears to hear. I will be citing scriptures from the Bible, the Vedas, and other holy books to illustrate my points. Please remember that this is just a point of view, nothing more. If it resonates with you, irritates, causes a shift in perception, then that is more than I could have hoped for.

Realise: **You** are the "second coming." You, beautiful soul, are who you have been waiting for. **You.**

This means you, me, we have to grow into full adulthood, take responsibility, and walk the talk. It's our time.

To quote the New Testament John 5:2-8:

"2Now there is in Jerusalem near the Sheep Gate a pool with five covered colonnades, which in Hebrew is called Bethesda. 3On these walkways lay a great number of the sick, the blind, the lame, and the paralyzed.

(Allegorical)

"5 One man there had been an invalid for thirty-eight years. 6 When Jesus saw him lying there and realized that he had spent a long time in this condition, He asked him, "Do you want to get well?"

(This is an important question. Do you WANT to get well? Ask yourself the same question.)

7"Sir," the invalid replied, "I have no one to help me into the pool when the water is stirred. While I am on my way, someone else goes in before me."

(Blaming others for missing his chances, self piteous, and low self esteem.)

8Then Jesus told him: "Get up, pick up your mat, and walk."

9Immediately the man was made well, and he picked up his mat and began to walk.

This means: THERE IS NOTHING WRONG WITH YOU! TAKE RESPONSIBILITY FOR YOURSELF AND WALK IN THE LIGHT OF CREATION.

Our journey to the Godhead started many eons ago and now, here we all are, ready to take a deeper and more intimate step toward the God inside of us. We will walk together as one people, united in the Spirit of truth. Have faith in God and trust. Trust the process. Trust God. The God within.

Let's examine the God within:

"Whoever dwells in the shelter of the Most High will rest in the shadow of the Almighty."

(The shelter of the most high is your pineal gland)

Image by Daisy Sheppard

"I WILL SAY OF THE LORD, "He is my refuge and my fortress, my God, in whom I trust."

Interpretation: Make the most high—your pineal gland—your dwelling, and you shall come to no harm. You shall see in advance all you need. Nothing will frighten you. You will be Divinely protected.

As you are here, I am presuming you already know what the pineal gland is and where it is located, but just to refresh your memory, here is a list of points to remember:

· The shape of the gland resembles a pine cone, hence its name. It is located in the epithalamus, near the centre of the brain. The symbol of the pinecone is universally used to signify the pineal gland.

· The pineal gland is not paired like other glands.

· French philosopher Descartes famously referred to the pineal gland as "The Seat of the Soul."

· The pineal gland's association with the metaphysical third eye allows it to be considered the organ of supreme universal connection.

· It is mentioned in the Old Testament and new (Bible), in Hindu, Buddhist, and most holy scriptures on the plane(t).

· All species have pineal glands, making us all spiritual beings, and most animals' pineal glands are larger than ours. We know they use their intuition to communicate with each other. My thoughts are that they "hear" the frequencies of others, their thoughts, intentions, and feelings. We do too, but some have lost this ability owing to stress, fatigue (adrenal), and the kind of disconnected lives we tend to live at this time.

· The pineal produces melatonin, a honey-coloured liquid hormone that helps regulate sleep and wakefulness and the circadian patterns that have broad effects on health (e.g.: too little or too much sleep). N.B.: The Land of milk and honey is symbolic of the pituitary and pineal glands and their hormone production (melatonin = honey-coloured hormone from the pineal and oxytocin = milky-coloured hormone from the pituitary).

· The pineal gland is also important in its influence on the endocrine glands and could be viewed as the "regulator of regulators."

· It is also thought that pineal functioning may play an important role in conditions deemed as mental illness such as schizophrenia and similar, connected conditions. (Ref: 1) This is why it is so important to decalcify the pineal and take good care of the "temple" (body).

· It's also important in regard to the function of the thyroid. (Ref: 2)

· The pineal body lies within the roof of the third ventricle, deep within the brain. Autopsy studies have shown that the average size of the pineal gland is similar to a grain of rice. The ventricles are fluid-filled spaces, and the third ventricle extends from the large lateral ventricles to the narrow cerebral aqueduct, passing between the two halves of the part of the brain called the diencephalon. ("Enter by the narrow path" — Mathew 7:13-14 is the narrow cerebral aqueduct.)

· It is located within an area called the epithalamus, just behind the thalamus and above the cerebellum, resting at the back of the brain near the brainstem. There is a small, fluid-filled pineal recess that projects into the stalk of the pineal body, allowing for the hormones it produces to more easily be diffused throughout the brain.

· Basically, it's in the middle of your head just like an aerial or radio receiver

1. It is not protected by the blood brain barrier.

· "Modern medical dissection has already discovered that the front section of the pineal gland is equipped with the **complete structure of a human eye**. Because it grows inside one's skull, it is thus said to be a vestigial organ (remnant of something formerly existing). Yet modern medicine has, after all, already recognized that there is an eye in the middle of the human brain." (Ref: 3)

· Scientists are still baffled as to why the pineal gland is photoreceptive. "That is to say, if there is a light-transducing passageway, a pineal gland is capable of detecting light. This can explain why photic suppression of pineal melatonin remained unaffected in mice genetically lacking retinal photoreceptors. There may exist a secret 'unknown light-transducing passageway' that allows the mammalian pineal gland to detect light directly." (Ref: 4)

I POSTULATE THAT SOME of the light that the pineal gland receives comes directly from source and is outside the visible spectrum. It therefore penetrates the skull more easily, rather like the way infrared wavelengths penetrate the skin down to the bone, or like hydrogen passing easily through metal. There is also the Tenth "hole" to consider.

The physical human body has nine physical openings: The two eyes, two nostrils, two ears, anus, genitals, and mouth. The tenth opening is known in Sikh terms as Dasam Duar and is metaphysical. This is purportedly the place where the infinite dwells and is the gate, "When opened, enables the vision of creator in mind." "The tenth gate is an experience not a physical phenomenon." (Ref: 5)

"When you have a receiver of any description, for it to work efficiently and pick up the wanted signal, it requires being shielded from random noise i.e. unwanted signals. It follows therefore, that the pineal gland might well be situated in the depths of the brain such that the aqueous matter around it acts as a shield. The wanted signal is ported along transparent glutinous matter (cerebral aqueduct) which runs adjacent to the pituitary gland and feeds the thalamus where the signal is possibly magnified. It might well be the case that the rods within the pineal are longer than those in the eyes because the frequency of reception is of a different wavelength." Lecaz. S, engineer. (Ref: 6)

Some people see more of the invisible spectrum e.g. blue light, the biofield, and other indescribable colours. It could be said that these are the resonances or frequencies that the pineal gland "sees" or perceives in a different way according to one's consciousness and vibration. I have hidden this ability all my life as it led to bullying and being called a witch on numerous occasions. Now, it's all being revealed on a global scale.

Currently, research is being led by Dan Winter training both children and adults to see without their eyes. The results are extremely interesting, especially for those who are a little sceptical. You can find his research in the list of references. (Ref: 7)

Beings of a lower vibration or density are unable to consciously perceive anything higher than their spectrum or vibratory range. This is a very useful type of protection.

In purchasing this book, you now have access to the pineal activation program (here is the link: https://bit.ly/ pinealactivationprogram1) where you can relax into a deeper, expanded state of consciousness, open your mind, inner hearing, heart, and soul, to an infinite love of our creator, who or whatever that may be for you.

Research began in the 1970s and 80s regarding how the pineal is affected by the external environment, including EMRs, TETRA masts, microwaves, and other energies or frequencies.

Research shows 5G and similar types of sonic radiation affect our whole body. The pineal is no exception. Please watch the video in Reference 8.

Let us take a look at exactly where the pineal gland sits. Also, let's look at "The Tree of Life" (Arbor Vitae) as seen in the video "It's time to wake up the trees." (Ref: 9)

Our pineal is right in the centre between the two hemispheres. It is the Godhead.

The fact that the pineal is a single organ and not paired is interesting because it has two inputs—like sensory pathways—and could be compared to a circuit board, where the pineal is the central controller for the neurological and hormonal systems of the body. It balances, regulates, and manages everything and is rather like an infinite, consciousness-expanding microchip. One might ask, "How can something so small do so much?" I am in awe. (Ref: 10) What an amazing creator we serve.

In the 'Pineal Gland Diagram' you can see a picture of the pineal from the dorsal viewpoint. It was when I saw this view of the pineal that I realised some interesting anthropomorphic representations e.g.: the story of Christ, the Ark of the Covenant, and the crown of thorns.

I heard a radio broadcast on BBC Radio 4 in 2018 by a neuroscientist who mentioned a newly discovered nerve in mice that circumnavigated the skull and is responsible for consciousness. I researched it and thought "that looks just like the crown of thorns." Interestingly, the scientists named it the crown of thorns. This led me to look more deeply at the brain and its parts. I remembered having the revelation that the Indian Gods represented states of consciousness and then had the idea to look them up, one by one and that's when it got really very interesting.

I saw that there were other parts of the brain that had been anthropomorphised and mythologised into stories, fables, and legends. The more I looked, the more I saw and continue to see. You can get the images clearly in my video "it's time to wake up the trees."

Chapter Two: The Sacred Secretion

———

The Bible is such a strange and fascinating book, full of weird and wonderful stories, allegories, wisdom, pain, suffering, ascension, love, astronomy, bigamy, incest, astrology, good and evil spirits, and prophets. Like a crucible of human consciousness, it acts like a spiritual map. If you take it all literally, you will find yourself in big trouble. It won't make sense. It has also been edited over the centuries and important books have been taken out, rewritten, badly translated, twisted out of all proportion, and misinterpreted but, for those who have eyes to see and ears to hear, it is absolutely incredible and there's still enough potent material in there to navigate your way to God without getting lost, if you take the time to really look. When my awakening came, I had studied scripture for seven years, suffered at the hands of ignorant pastors who took everything literally, and had endured the hardest time on the physical plane leading to two near death experiences. I learned the deeper meaning of faith, forgiveness, and true love as a result. I got stuck in the book of Genesis for three and a half years until the true meaning of the Garden of Eden was revealed. Following that, everything else then fell into place.

So you might ask, what is the meaning of the Tree of Life, the Garden of Eden, Adam and Eve, the "Snake" in the garden, the crucifixion and ascension? Perhaps this is relevant to your journey. How does this compare to other faiths or expressions of the Divine Creator?

Let us begin with Genesis.

The Garden of Eden is a representation of your brain and body and all its contents, as seen in my video "It's time to wake up the trees." (Ref: 9) In the video you will see visual representations and a clear explanation of what I mean by this.

Each part of your brain and body is represented by rivers, tributaries, mountains, supernatural winged creatures, and other anthropomorphic beings from Angels, stairways to heaven (the spine or Jacob's ladder), to elephants personified as Ganesh (which is the back of the brain or cerebellum), trees (the Arbor Vitae), sacred fruit (pineal), and the twelve Apostles (twelve cranial nerves). The ancient ones knew this wisdom but it became hidden, occult, occluded from the masses as the "church" misused the information and led innocent lambs to their own slaughter, enslaving them in worthless spiritual, mental, and physical poverty, condemning them to perpetual spiritual slumber—that is, until now.

The true meaning of Christ is anointing oil. It originates from the Greek word. It seems so ridiculous to see people pouring oil over themselves in a church, believing that it is going to raise their consciousness or by worshiping in front of cross with no innernstanding of what it actually symbolises, everything it is going to transform. Everything religious has been externalised although the Bible clearly states that Christ and the sacred secretion is within. (Reference 17) The misinterpretation of this incredible, natural, divine process has been personified and instead of self-realisation and ascension, people are encouraged to look for an external saviour who takes all the responsibility from them. The truth is, when we awaken to what the Christ is, although the pain of what we call sin may weigh heavy, through this sacred process we are able to purge and continually ascend to higher frequencies and a greater love.

Christ or Chrism means consecrated oil as derived from Greek chriein "to anoint".

Jesus (Iesous) when literally translated from Greek means "Hail Zeus." The name Jesus didn't even exist before the 4th century.

"It is known that the Greek name endings with sus, seus, and sous were attached by the Greeks to names and geographical areas as means to give honour to their supreme deity, Zeus." (Reference 18)

I find it interesting that this kind of deception has fooled the masses into a misplaced version of true honour and worship of the Divine, both internally and externally. I personally have no problem with worshiping the Sun, Moon, and Stars But the stories in the Bible, The Bagavad Gita, Quran, and most other religious scriptures have literally become Gospel, taken literally, totally losing the actual meaning of them. As a result, we have religions of superstition and ignorance perpetuating the same low vibrational habits of killing, poverty, hierarchy, foolishness, and pain or false highs and states of bliss that cannot be sustained owing to the fact that not everyone can spend their lives sitting under a Bodhi tree. The route to natural enlightenment has been commercially blocked. It's almost as if the electric energy created by human beings all believing particular things is harvested by a greedy few who have their own, hidden agenda, but perhaps I am merely musing?

Now is the time to recover who we truly are, awaken our spirits, and rise. You might call this Global Ascension. We are here at this time in history to break the pattern of aeons of indoctrination and set ourselves and all the captives free—or rather, those who wish to be liberated. If you are here, then you know why and what you have been called to do, regardless of your brand of faith (e.g.: Sikh, Christian, Jew, Moslem, Agnostic, etc.).

For me, it took over fifty years to step into who I truly am, but that's another story for another book.

I marvel at the magnificent creation that we are. So beautiful, each and every one of us.

Perhaps take a moment to give thanks to our incredible Creator and the Divine Creation of all that is before embarking on the next part of our journey. Could it be that as our minds and hearts have expanded, we have quantum jumped back in time and affected our future? I wonder? One way or another, the truth will out.

Temple of God

In the book of Genesis (Bible: Genesis 1) we read about creation where the waters were separated from the firmament (the waters above) and how Hu-mans came into existence. Some people take this literally, but I'd like to think that we can take a wider viewpoint. Whether or not you think that the omitted Book of Enoch reveals a flat Earth with waters above and below the firmament, or perhaps you are more inclined to see it as quantum foam, the poetic language does invite inspection. For the sake of argument, let us put down our ideas for a moment and examine these scripts from a different perspective.

Definition: Hu means spirit. Human = Spirit-(wo)man. Wo = short for womb.

NB: Sufis chant Hu as a mantra, as do other practices (e.g.: Ekankar, Sikhism). Hu is the ancient name for God in many different cultures. It also clearly defines the musical harmonic series when chanted. (Ref:19)

We innerstand that sound creates form (Ref: 11) and remember, in the Bible it states that God "spoke" the world into being:

"And God said, "Let there be light," and there was light." Genesis1:1

"In the beginning was the Word, and the Word was with God, and the Word was God." John 1:1

All is sound, light, and vibrating frequencies held together by consciousness, i.e. that which is aware. The awareness of awareness. The harmonic and dissonant frequencies we recognise as musical notes, thoughts, emotions, and ideas create the symphony of life and we resonate accordingly, sometimes in tune and sometimes, as the jazz song suggests "Decifinado," slightly out of tune. Even our hormonal secretions indicate our state of being from cortisol to melatonin. We "speak" life into being through our thoughts, words, intentions, consciousness, and it could be said, our unconsciousness and collective consciousness.

The colours we perceive within our spectrum are all vibrating and have their own frequencies. New colours outside of our perception are higher vibrations, unseen to most. The higher our vibration, the more we are able to perceive. At this time on Earth, the ability to sense the vibration of colours without seeing them with our eyes, through feeling or audibly is a natural skill that is being restored.

Regarding our subconscious, from the time we are born, the programming starts in the form of positive and negative ideas (e.g.: heaven and hell) creating conscious and subconscious beliefs accompanied by suffering and fears, which may or may not become triggered and play out in the physical world as life dramas or traumas. Through tuning in (literally) to our deepest super nature, we can bring these programs into full consciousness and see them for what they are, releasing any frequencies that are no longer useful in the same way we excrete in the physical world, like a sort of emotional, mental, and spiritual excretory system.

In Hebrews it states in verse 11:3, "By faith we understand that the universe was created by the word of God, so that what is seen was not made out of things that are visible." Indicating a linear timeline, a future and a past of things that were created from the unseen, this Biblical statement is a clarion call to faith. Let us take faith as a frequency of inner knowing and trust and the unseen into seen as the manifestation of the frequencies of thought, emotion and experience. However, from a quantum perspective, we know that there are countless timelines and multiverses with infinite potential and possibilities. The universe becomes the multiverse as we grow in awareness and beyond.

The invisible realms, or spirit realms, are where all things are conceived and happen first, outside of linear time, in a multidimensional intelligence. (Please watch the video explanation of the dimensions as a reference point. (Ref: 12))

It could be said that we only "see," or "perceive," as far as our consciousness allows. As we expand through conscious spiritual practice on a daily basis, we are able to see more, seeing into what we term as the "invisible," or spiritual realms beyond our three-dimensional reality into the immensity of God's creation, speaking it into our being as we go.

Let's define dimensions. They are literally angles or "angels." This is our sacred geometry, anthropomorphised so we can perceive it all in three and four dimensions, therefore, angles become angels, the Cerebrum become Cherubim, the Hippocampus becomes a horse and so on. A combination of shapes (degrees) creates resonances or dissonances. For example, one's birth chart creates a geometric shape plotting where the stars are at the time of your birth. Therefore, it could be said that if seen in three or four dimensions, the geometric shape, or angles, create your unique "resonance," which then changes and fluctuates throughout the timeline.

A three-dimensional representation of a birth chart is a more visual way of comprehending the angles of resonance within one's own field. The geometric angles create their own sonic frequencies and one can see how this harmony of life potentially plays out with all its resonance and dissonance as our journey through this timeline progresses. These are all musical frequencies that could be measured in Hertz if there were equipment sensitive enough to do it. Remember, every room or enclosed space has its own resonance, and this translates from the microcosm to the macrocosm, the centre point being the Sun. Instead of looking at astrology in two dimensions, perhaps we might examine the resonances that the external angles create internally? Every constellation, universe, multiverse, and galaxy is within us, after all. Our innerverse.

It is said that the temple of God was made in the image of God. Of course, the temple of God is us. We *are* it. We are the living embodiment of our creator. The only separations are the ones we put there, consciously or unconsciously, according to our conditioning.

As living, sentient temples, perhaps we need to know how to keep ourselves "clean" and "holy" so the presence of the Divine (photon) can dwell easily within us. No one likes a dirty house or bed to sleep in. Even radio transmitters and receivers have to be kept in good condition in order to avoid sonic interference. Bearing in mind that life in the twenty-first century is quite dense and low in vibration from the contaminated food we eat to the endless microwaves and sonic frequencies spewed out into the atmosphere, taking time to keep physically, emotionally, hermeneutically, mentally, and spiritually clean is essential.

The first place to start in this process is with a detox to clean our temples.

The Detox:

Please **consult your health practitioner** for the best way for you to detox. We are all unique so it's best to work out what is best for you at this time.

Here are a few pointers:

- Daniel Fast (just veggies, no sugar, no alcohol, no caffeine)

· Intermittent Fasting (16 hours between main meals e.g.: Not eating after 2pm)

· Partial Fast (once a week)

· Hard Core Water Fast for the experienced warriors (please used distilled or purified water only. A distiller can be easily found via all the usual channels.)

Pineal detox aids:

· Clean slate (Ref 13),

· C60,

· spirulina,

· greens and supergreens,

· sprouted seeds,

· MMS/CDL (Chlorine dioxide),

· Don't forget the humble apple; organic cider vinegar is excellent

Please do your own research as to what is best for your own system via your practitioner.

It's important to detox emotionally, mentally, and spiritually as well as physically. That means taking good care of what you're doing with your eyes, your mind, your heart, and your voice. Pay attention to areas of toxicity and let them go. I have found a very good exercise is to spend twenty minutes a day doing a spiritual visualization detox. In the past, I have found a place internally where I go to empty the spiritual, emotional, and mental trash. I don't like to be prescriptive, so the best thing is to find your own way of "emptying" and cleaning up. It could be as simple as taking the trash bin out and watching the refuse collectors take it away.

Some Pointers

· Examine what you are focusing upon. Cease any visual temptations of a lustful nature.

· Examine your emotional patterns and responses. Face up. Forgive and let go.

· Forgive everyone for everything. Un-forgiveness will stop you from reaching the God-head. Think of forgiveness as a harmonious frequency or vibration and un-forgiveness as a discord.

Atomic Focus

From a quantum perspective, that which we focus upon comes into being:

Proverbs 23:7: "For as he thinketh in his heart, so is he."

Even Tony Robbins says: "energy flows where attention goes."

In quantum physics, wherever you focus your attention, atoms appear. (Ref 14) Remembering that all is frequency and vibration, that means thoughts are also particles and waves. How many times have you noticed stinking thinking? Just being around certain people can be a downer. If our lives are not functioning well, we might need to focus on things of a higher vibration. It could be said that focus itself is part of the circuit. We could use the word at-tension (attention). When we pay attention, we notice. We bring our lens to view whatever it is. We observe and we know that when something is observed it behaves differently. Let us have a look at where our attention is focused and how we are acting or playing out our lives. We're all works in progress, and one could say we are all tested based on where our individual weaknesses lie. Why? One might ask: Why do things go wrong?

If we are mirrors of God (made in the image of) as we become more conscious, we reconcile to ourselves, realising who and what we are as the God particle, seeing and experiencing ourselves in relation to our other selves (i.e. everyone else), adding to the incredible, infinite consciousness that we are and perhaps, learning true, unconditional love. God is love and love is God. Truly comprehending this explains almost everything there is to know.

As I stood in the garden of my mind, I pondered over and over and over again, the meaning of the book of Genesis. I visualised every bit of creation and the story of Adam and Eve, the tree of life, the fall, the talking snake, the land of Eden, and tried to comprehend it. Very, very slowly, things started to unfold. I began to see that Genesis is the greatest love story of all time. I marvelled at the universe's conception — mirrored in the formation of life in the womb. How the growth of a child inside the mother is replicated in separating the waters, and that the foetus goes through every part of the evolutionary timeline from the atom to the human being.

Uni (one) Verse (Spoken word).

Adam (Atom)

Eve (Before)

Atom and Before.

Amen, Ammon, Adam, Atum, and Atom are all the same word.

THE LAND OF MILK AND Honey

Exodus 3:8: "So I have come down to deliver them from the power of the Egyptians, and to bring them up from that land to a good and spacious land, to a land flowing with milk and honey."

Part of my deeper spiritual awakening started when I questioned the meaning of the land of milk and honey while reading the scriptures (Ref: 15). I just could not see that God would be that literal; I got stuck trying to figure it out for quite a while. Then I heard the inner voice say: "Research the pineal gland" and there, I found my answers.

To Recap

The pineal gland creates a honey-coloured liquid and the pituitary a milky-coloured substance; joined together they become the cerebral-spinal fluid. This fluid has a monthly cycle related to the time of your birth and the moon passing through your native sun sign. (You can find this information easily on a website called :Moontracks. (Ref: 15))

It is released via the Claustrum (Santa Claus—trum) and descends thirty-three degrees down to the sacrum via the solar plexus, where it combines with the Holy Spirit, or Prana, or Source Energy. It then enters the celiac plexus or "Bethlehem," which means house of bread. The combination of the Holy Spirit and the cerebral spinal fluid creates the "seed."

This seed must then find the sacral pump in order to be raised back up the body, once again through the solar plexus, the cardiac plexus, and up the thirty-three vertebrae of the spine, ascending through all the energy centres, crossing the vagus nerve for two and a half days when the moon enters our sun-sign, where it is "crucified," or purified, refined, and potentised, and then returned to the pineal, where enlightenment, or meeting God face to face, takes place.

On a personal note, I have found that during my two and a half days of refining every month, I am **severely** tempted and usually put through the mangle on every level. Over the years, I suffered a lot and lost the oil because I was pushed to my absolute limit and lacked discipline. My hope is that I have broken through this limitation and that I will become more adept at **preserving the oil**. In fact, I have had to make big inner and outer changes, in order to stay in alignment with the God, I am, within. I hope that this knowledge will encourage you to do the same.

My personal longing for deep peace both inside and out is stronger than my desire for carnal relationships and physical possessions. However, it was the attachment to having or not having them that created a blockage, which through working closely with my friend Vinny M Grant, has been rectified.

To make the vagus time (monthly crucifixion) go a little more smoothly, here are some pointers:

- Resist temptation during your two and a half days and be mindful of what is happening to you.

- KNOW you will be tempted and pushed to your absolute limit. The lower energies (enemy within) do not want ascension to happen so don't forget.

- Don't lose your cool (like I did) and blow a month's worth of discipline! (James 4:7: "Submit yourselves, then, to God. Resist the devil, and he will flee from you.")

- As you go through the month, go gently and with awareness.

- Pay attention to what is issuing from your mouth.

- The Christ teaching gave us two laws:

1. Love God with all of your heart, mind, body, soul, and spirit; and

2. Love your neighbour as yourself.

All else is contained within these two laws. If you can master just these two, then you will have cracked it.

To clarify, refrain from:

- pride,

- greed,

- wrath,

- envy,

- lust,

- gluttony,

- and sloth.

Rejoice in:

- Love

- Joy

- Peace

- Patience

- Kindness

- Goodness

- Faithfulness

- Gentleness

- Self control

These qualities are the beautiful fruits of the spirit of which we can eat bountifully.

Please see the link to a new piece of music (Ref: 16) with the sonic frequency for each energy centre. It's a daily meditation in preparation for the ascension of the sacred secretion also known as "raising the Chrism," "raising the Christ," or Kundalini in the Hindu faith.

Practice your meditation, sonic alignment, affirmations, or visualisations daily, and be consistent. Be strict with yourself but don't punish yourself if you slip up. The most important time for this is your two and a half days.

The story of the ten virgins speaks of the Holy oil. (Mathew 25:1-13). It is very clear from this story that it is essential to save the oil, to not be distracted, and to connect with the "Bridegroom" (i.e. Creator), who will eventually show up at the right moment.

1 "At that time the kingdom of heaven will be like ten virgins who took their lamps and went out to meet the bridegroom. 2 Five of the virgins were foolish, and five were wise. 3 When the foolish ones took their *lamps, they did not take extra*266[1] *olive oil with them. 4 But the wise ones took flasks of olive oil with their lamps. 5 When the bridegroom was delayed a long time,*267[2] *they all became drowsy and fell asleep. 6 But at midnight there was a shout, 'Look, the bridegroom is here! Come out to meet him.' 7 Then all the virgins woke up and trimmed their lamps. 8 The foolish ones said to the wise, 'Give us some of your oil, because our lamps are going out.' 9 'No,' they replied. 'There won't be enough for you and for us. Go instead to those who sell oil and buy some for yourselves.' 10 But while they had gone to buy it, the bridegroom arrived, and those who were ready went inside with him to the wedding banquet. Then the door was shut. 11 Later, the other virgins came too, saying, 'Lord, lord! Let us in!' 12 But he replied, 'I tell you the truth, I do not know you!' 13 Therefore stay alert, because you do not know the day or the hour."*

1. https://bible.org/seriespage/26-ten-virgins-what-it-means-be-ready-matthew-251-13%2523P2672_935884

2. https://bible.org/seriespage/26-ten-virgins-what-it-means-be-ready-matthew-251-13%252523P2673_936134

Chapter 3

―――

A Revelation

Now, I would like to go into a little more depth regarding the energy centres, the cerebral spinal fluid, the "Book of Revelation" in the Bible, and Hindu Gods to perhaps bring a new or slightly different perspective regarding the meaning of these scripts and symbols. This novel observation derives from questioning the generic interpretation of all the above. As I began to see through the symbols, my perception universally changed as if by osmosis, and I could not un-see what was in front of me. I am not convinced by the reasons for such universal occlusion in the scripts and wonder why things should be hidden from view in such a clumsy and deceptive way. The truth is eternal and has no copyright, so why confuse people with such limiting misinterpretations? It's almost as if some part of us is playing a game with another part, trying to arrest our own spiritual development. What is astounding, is that the ubiquitous knowledge we all feel so comfortable with is so partial. Hasn't anyone noticed? There are pieces missing all over the place. It shocks me that people sit hypnotised in their pews on a Sunday or stuck in some Yogic position with their leg wrapped around their neck searching for an external truth, spoon-fed to them by some guru or pastor. As far as I can see, the only way to grasp the complete truth of who we are is by going "in," and trusting what we see, no matter how far out it seems.

In this life, I have devoted my time to making music and following the call of my spirit. Looking back, it might have been quicker to find the answers I was looking for if I had studied anthropology instead of living it. However, I don't regret a single moment of apparent fruitless searching since I have experienced everything first-hand, which has enhanced the development of my internal compass and bullshit detector, for which I am truly grateful. I can smell a lie a mile away these days. I also apply all of this to myself as I have been accused of being an excitable horse who charges off in the wrong direction, wind in my mane and tail, gossamer wings at the ready only to reach a cliff edge. So far, I have managed to jump the ravines and allow Pegasus to be born, but there have been some dicey moments along the way.

Upon researching the seven churches, I didn't have much more to go on than a hunch; some things have been a bit of a stretch. At the very least, it might cause you, the reader, to perceive things differently, or disagree with me, or take it further. That's what it's about. I'll be pleased to think that this might open a discussion or internal dialogue.

Please note there are many more energy centres than the seven represented here. In my opinion, these seven are elementary. The occluded knowledge inside all of us might tell you that there are an infinite number of energy centres inside and outside the body. What is represented in the Bible and other scripts is, in my opinion, only partial information and, at best, is introductory.

However, let me begin with the last book of the Bible written by "John" and known as Revelation. In my humble opinion, this book has nothing to do with "the end of the world," and everything to do with our own personal ascension(s). It has been turned upside down and inside out, weaponised, and totally misconstrued into a religious cult, which has nothing to do with anything except power over and control of unquestioning, dumbed-down populations who are looking for a saviour and refuse to take responsibility for themselves. That time is now over.

"The Revelation of Jesus Christ, which God gave Him to show His servants—things which must shortly take place. And He sent and signified it by His angel to His servant John, 2 who bore witness to the word of God, and to the testimony of Jesus Christ, to all things that he saw. 3 Blessed is he who reads and those who hear the words of this prophecy, and keep those things which are written in it; for the time is near." (Revelation 1)

Let us take a deeper look at this passage. I don't intend to rewrite the Bible, but to shine a light on the meaning of some of the words:

"The revelation of Jesus Christ, which God gave him"

Metaphysically translated, this means: The revealing of truth to the anointed one, Jesus, AKA Yeshua, Iēsoús, Jehoshua (which means Yahweh saves / Yahweh is salvation, or in the Greek, Hail Zeus!). Taking into consideration that we are all anointed, all have Christ within, (cerebral spinal fluid and Christ consciousness), it means that this "revelation" is for everybody who is on the Spiritual path, seeking God's face.

More explicitly: The revealing of truth to the anointed one, (whom) Yahweh saves, to show others (his servants) the things that must surely come to pass on the path of enlightenment. The resonance channeled and written down (signified) by His servant John (which means Yahweh has been gracious). (Ref: 31)

When I was fourteen, I read the book of Revelation and realised that it was a map, a clear map written for the God-seeker and for all those on the spiritual path. It's a spiritual aid or reference point in this illusory world. It tells you what to expect on each level of the journey and how to handle it. It is also written in code or parable form so only those who have eyes to see and ears to hear can see what is hidden in plain sight.

It is not a prophecy of the End Times unless we make it so. We do not have to fulfil this misinterpretation of scripture. Maintaining the willful misinterpretation is not helpful to anyone or anything. This interpretation is a lie, a self-fulfilling prophecy written by the controllers, and implemented by people who know no better. It's not even rational to suppose that the end of the world will cast unworthy souls into a fiery pit for eternity along with everything and everyone else who has sinned. It doesn't fit into the Christian paradigm. We speak life into being (sound creates form) so the more we speak it out, the more it will manifest perpetually until we stop the nonsense. Frankly, it doesn't fit with the infinite Divine intelligence and unconditionally loving God within, but more with a wrathful, vengeful, unforgiving, small-minded-humanistic cabal approach. What we believe in on a quantum level, creates the perception to achieve and so therefore, the real question here is: what is the frequency of belief?

From the four horsemen of the apocalypse to the seventh seal, Revelation does exactly what it says on the tin, it reveals. For example, there are four cranial nerves in the medulla, four structures on the lateral side, four above the pons and four motor nuclei in the midline. I postulate that the four horsemen in the book of Revelation are the four Cranial Nerves in the Medulla.

The Cranial nerves in the Medulla:

1. Glossopharyngeal
2. Vagus
3. Spinal accessory
4. Hypoglossal

The Seven Churches

9 I, John, [f]both your brother and companion in the tribulation and kingdom and patience of Jesus Christ, was on the island that is called Patmos for the word of God and for the testimony of Jesus Christ. 10 I was in the Spirit on the Lord's Day, and I heard behind me a loud voice, as of a trumpet, 11 saying, [g] "I am the Alpha and the Omega, the First and the Last," and, "What you see, write in a book and send it to the seven churches [h]which are in Asia: to Ephesus, to Smyrna, to Pergamos, to Thyatira, to Sardis, to Philadelphia, and to Laodicea."

In the following, I seek to cross reference the meaning of these words and unlock a deeper comprehension of the self — body, mind, and spirit — and expand upon the ubiquitous perception of the meaning of the seven churches.

Patmos — derived noun πατημα (patema), meaning either step, or that which is stepped on, that which is trodden. This in turn describes either grapes or olives that are trodden for their juice and oil, or else dung and refuse that gets trodden underfoot.

In my opinion, Patmos speaks of a state of consciousness, not of the island in Greece where John is said to have written the last book of the Bible — although it could be said that it might be both. It alludes to an internal crushing or suffering to create the "oil" or "juice" of revelation. The pain of spiritual sacrifice to reach a deeper state of awareness, of one treading one's own inner dung underfoot, symbolises the overcoming of the lower nature.

I recall from my days in Buddhist practice that the lotus blossom begins life in the muddy pool and pushes through the dirt to rise into the light, perfect and unsullied, just like our Spirits, in an aesthetic symbol of ascension. Interestingly, French scientists have based a non-stick spoon on the atomic structure of a lotus leaf. This is known as The Lotus Effect or superhydrophobic surfaces. (Ref: 32) Our Spirit, the infinite energy we all are, is untouchable and pure. It is only in our physical form that we really physically feel the emotions of pain, sorrow, suffering, and hate manifested as the apparency of something believable. In the words of my American friend Professor Alan Rice: "Don't kick shit cos it sticks to your boot." (Prof. Rice, who has a brain the size of a planet, worked out how to turn radio-active nuclear waste back into organic matter among many other achievements, has a lot more to offer than just the above coarse idiom, but his words have released me from many an emotional trap over the years.) Ref:31.1

It could be said that John received his revelations following a crushing or sacrifice in the physical realm. Perhaps if there was a John, and he actually was on the island of Patmos at the time, the inner world or supernatural world reflected in the natural — or perhaps he was elsewhere. In my experience, I expect it was both, as these things usually have a wonderful symmetry to them.

The first church or temple he wrote about was Ephesus. Bear in mind that church is also another word for temple. (Ref: 33, 34) The Indo-European derivation of church is "to swell," or a vault or hole. It could be said that this directly correlates with an energy centre.

Ephesus—Root chakra / energy centre "The church that needed to repent." But why?

Definitions: In his *Hittite Etymological Dictionary*, Jaan Puhvel (Ref: 35) explains the Hittite element appa to mean "'behind, back' in a spatial, but uniformly 'after' in a temporal sense," and relates it to common words in Sanskrit (apatyam, meaning offspring; apara, meaning later) and the Greek (επι, epi, meaning on or upon; οπις, opis, meaning looking back).

The name Apasa and thus Ephesus would thus literally mean Later Place. At the end of a river, it was called Place Very Much at the Back and named in the sense of Lands' End.

A place at the end of a river i.e., the Perineum or Sacrum, is the place at the end of the spine.

In *Biblical Names* (Ref: 20) the meaning of the name Ephesus is: Desirable. Let's take away any demonisation of the body and see this area for what it is. Some people have anthropomorphised this into some devilish forms which, as far as I can see, tell a very different story to the one we are living or at odds with. As we are now coming into mass awakening, perhaps it could be said that we can free ourselves from the ignorance of the past. Why would you tell a fearful story except to assert control over those who hear it? Perhaps the story correlates to how positive and negative energy flow and that the junction box can cause a malfunction or burn out if not properly taken care of. Perhaps it's time to revisit the scripts with all the knowledge we have at our fingertips through information technology.

To the Church in Ephesus

2 "To the angel[a] of the church in Ephesus write: These are the words of him who holds the seven stars in his right hand and walks among the seven golden lampstands. 2 I know your deeds, your hard work and your perseverance. I know that you cannot tolerate wicked people, that you have tested those who claim to be apostles but are not and have found them false. 3 You have persevered and have endured hardships for my name and have not grown weary.4 Yet I hold this against you: You have forsaken the love you had at first. 5 Consider how far you have fallen! Repent and do the things you did at first. If you do not repent, I will come to you and remove your lampstand from its place. 6 But you have this in your favour: You hate the practices of the Nicolaitans, which I also hate.7 Whoever has ears, let them hear what the Spirit says to the

churches. To the one who is victorious, I will give the right to eat from the tree of life, which is in the paradise of God.

We have defined Ephesus as the "place at the back" or end of the river. So, what does it mean regarding the seven lamp stands and stars? It could be said that this relates to the seven well-known energy centres of the body. The right hand symbolises sovereignty and the right hemisphere of the brain, therefore the seven stars held in the right hand would be one who has fully awakened and overcome the genetic memory/programs, reigning as a sovereign being over his or her earthly temple.

And let's not forget the constellation of the Seven Sisters, also known as The Pleiades. There are many myths and legends surrounding these seven sisters and they are universal, from the 'Orinigee' (Aboriginee) nation to Greek stories of old.

The question here is how does this relate to us, our outer body and inner spiritual body, and the body of our beloved Mother Earth, knowing that everything is connected?

I am reminded of how the stars sing. It's almost as if they are singing our sunrise into existence with an exquisite melody, singing life into being.

"When the morning stars sang together, and all the sons of God shouted for joy?"

(Job 38:7 English Standard Bible)

The seven stars are within us as we harmonise with the whole universe and together as multiverses, a symphony of beauty and truth, the dissonances always resolving to the fundamental, eventually. (Ref: 21)

I AM REMINDED THAT the symbol for Christ is a fish. Ichthus. Some New Agers would say this is symbolic of the Piscean Age and are relieved to be in the new age of Aquarius. However, I'd like to remind them of a few things: (Ref: 22) Christ / Chrism is oil, which is the cerebral spinal fluid created by the pituitary and pineal glands. The symbol of the fish is used to signify the raising of the Chrism, which can be perceived as the "seed" or sperm, or "fish." It germinates or is birthed in the celiac plexus or house of bread—also known as "Bethlehem."

The fish is one of the most important symbols for wealth

The fish symbol is known as the word 'ichthus' or 'ichthys' in Greek mysthology. It was an emblem for the followers of Christianity. The early believers found a way to make an acronym with using the first letters of the word. It's spelled as ΙΧΘΥΣ. The first letter stands for 'Jesus'. The second one stands for 'Christos', while the third is for 'God'. The fourth letter stands for 'Son' and the last one represents 'Savior'.

and fortune in the Asian cultures. It is offered to newly wed couples as a symbol of fertility, devotion, abundance, and good fortune. Koi in particular symbolise determination and courage owing to their ability to climb waterfalls and fast-flowing streams. In Japan, the Koi symbolise the Samurai Warrior.

In Buddhism, the fish (two of them) is one of the "Eight Auspicious Signs" symbolising happiness, as fish move freely in the water without restriction. They also symbolise longevity, as Koi live on average between twenty and fifty years. The longest-lived koi fish was a female named Hanako. She lived to be approximately 226 years old.

FUN FISH FACTS:

· Fish are cold-blooded and can't control their body temperature. Fish can feel pain.

· They have a good sense of taste, sight, and touch.

· Many fish taste without opening their mouth.

· Whale shark is the largest fish and they can grow to fifty feet long.

· Trigger fish can swim backward.

· If a goldfish is kept in a dark room it will lose its colour.

· The Egyptian tale of the Tilapia fish symbolises protection (the female fish protects her young in her mouth) and virility.

· In the Biblical scripts (Mathew 17:24), Peter caught a tilapia fish with a coin in its mouth. It could be said that this symbolises the internal work Peter had to do to reach inner freedom, where through the raising of the oil within he would reach the land of milk and honey (awakened state of consciousness or Christ consciousness) and all would be provided for naturally. The coin was specifically there to pay taxes. In my own life I have found that coming closer to an awakened state and living by faith and not by sight leads me to God's provision, where all is given freely.

THERE IS THE LEGEND the Nommos (Ref: 23) to whom the Dogon tribe give reverence in their culture, believing that these beings (or guardians) who were half-human half-fish, came from the star Sirius or Dog Star.

Some say that the Nommos were the offspring of the "fallen angels" or Nephilim who, according to the book of Enoch, mated with every living thing on the earth. These hybrids, according to the scripts, were part of "the fall" (so called) and contaminated human DNA, resulting in the evil characteristics now found in human beings today. This is just a postulate and might not be true. The place to look for the answer is within.

The story sounds strangely familiar: "The Nommo divided his body among men to feed them; that is why it is also said that as the universe "had drunk of his body," the Nommo also made men drink. He gave all his life principles to human beings."

"The Nommo was crucified and resurrected and in the future will again visit the Earth, this time in human form. Later he will assume his amphibious form and will rule the world from the waters." (Ref: 24)

Ultimately, perhaps the most important thing is to realise that the stories of demons and devils are red herrings (excuse the pun) in relation to our beautiful energy centres and who we truly are. We are not who we have been told we are, and this goes for all scripts and "religions" telling us that we are evil, enslaving us into thinking we are good-for-nothing wretches with nothing to live for. No.

Are there so-called demons? Are there negative energies? Of course, and partly because we think them into being or personify them, co-creating an agreed upon reality. We must only look at dissonances in music to find that the forms they create are aberrated and ugly. What purpose do they serve? Why, to wake us up and eventually bring us into union with God, the I am presence within us all.

We know that energy can be positive or negative and this is reflected in our own bodies. Our energy centres can, of course, be used or mis-used for the growth or demise of ourselves and others. It could be said that as we live in the apparency of duality; we have "choice" and, as we become more aware of our energy and others', we are able to make better choices and discern the invisible realm. Can we see energy? No. Energy is like the wind in the trees, we only see the effect of it.

We move energy with our intention, our bodies, souls, in all we think, do, and speak. Our actions are the latent effect of things already thought of or done outside of the physical realm. Ask yourself: "what is energy?" And "what is my energy doing right now?" We are electric beings, and our energy comes from source, in whichever way you wish to personify that. Wayne Dyer mentions the words source and sorcery, which made me chuckle and think about the Magi and magic. The demonisation of truth through words and symbols disempowers people unless they choose to look beyond the surface.

The root chakra (Ephesus in the scripture) is where you feel your connection to Earth and your sacral chakra. This is where the life force and sexual energy is rooted, manifested as the sexual organs and libido. It is situated at the perineum. In Vedic symbology, it is represented by an upside-down triangle showing the flow of energy toward the earth. This also fits with the shape of the rectum which, according to some, looks very much like a point of earth in a circuit board.

The electrical symbol for earth:

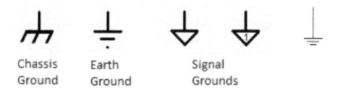

The symbol for the root chakra:

Notice the earth / ground symbol within it. Infact this symbol is used in all the chakras. Although the downward pointing triangle is currently interpreted as feminine energy and the opposite masculine, I postulate that this is in alignment with the electrical

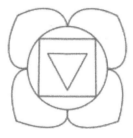

energy of our bodies.

Please see the you tube video reference in 'It's time to wake up the trees Part Two' at 05:54 mins for the image of Kali. (Ref: 24.1) The myths around her tell an interesting story. Notice the shape of the tongue and the rectum seen in the central image.

It could be said that the blue Gods/Goddesses represent the veinous system and other Gods and Deities might represent the arteries, lymphatic, and neurological systems.

Traditionally, the energy associated with the root is that of earth; its sonic frequency in a person is often close to the musical note of E, F, or G in the musical scale. The tone of F is approximately 174 Hz and is used for pain relief. If the note F is the fundamental, then middle C would be 528 Hz at the heart, which correlates both with the energy centres, notes resonating in the windpipe, and the harmonic series where the 5th is heard easily in relation to the root. (Ref: 21)

HOWEVER, EACH PERSON resonates at different frequencies according to their geometric shape as well as where they place their attention, consciousness, or subconscious load. Also, according to the research of Harvard Professor Gil Alterovitz, we each have a unique blood-song. (Ref: 25)

It could be said that the meaning of the Ephesus scripture is the energetic disconnection with the Divine Mother or Earth resulting in a feeling of complacency, forsaking the love once felt. The root is all about feeling safe and connected to the ground, like the roots of a tree reaching deep into the soil. Without this connection and love at the root, faithfulness (one of the seven spirits of God) is eroded, and in its place, fear, disorientation, and insecurity unmoor you.

Whether the root energy is strong and unmanageable for some (especially in the highly charged) or weak for others, effort is needed to maintain spiritual, mental, emotional, and physical balance. It could be said that too much energy in this area can result in a very controlling nature and too little presents as fear and insecurity causing inaction and no drive. That's a bit simplistic, but you get the point.

The comprehension of the divine masculine and feminine is mostly missing from our Western culture, causing a mass emasculation, disempowerment of both sexes, and lack of self-control resulting in the use pornography and the sexual abuse of men, women, and children.

"Isn't it ironic that the Catholic church is facing the requirement of repentance in regard to the rampant sexual abuse its representatives perpetrated on its adherents." (Ref: 27)

I couldn't agree more!

The ancient initiation rites have been squandered and our history removed, leaving us disorientated and disconnected from our true nature. We have lost comprehension of who we are and where we came from. (Dis meaning dissonance or dissonant frequencies.) The occult knowledge has been kept and misused by the so-called elite, and the written version is probably in storage in a Vatican vault of some sort. However, all is not lost because it's also written in our DNA. All we have to do is reach for it and it can be revived and restored.

To quote Steve Lecaz, scientist / engineer: "It can be no coincidence that below the root chakra lies the Earth to which connect our feet and which in turn, all other bodily senses play against in an exquisite counterpoise."

The energy centres are numerous and are like self-charging batteries, resonating at different frequencies from low Hertz to high Hertz, root to crown. The energy centres are impedance changers. Bill Donahue's research covers this subject brilliantly. To see a short clip, please view the second video "It's time to wake up the trees part two." (Ref: 27)

NB: There are many techniques for balancing our energy centres or chakras. A list of links can be seen on my website's members' page, and you can take your pick. www.itstimetowakeupthetrees.com[1]

To the Church in Smyrna

8 "To the angel of the church in Smyrna write: These are the words
    of him who is the First and the Last, who died and came to life
    again. 9 I know your afflictions and your poverty—yet you are
rich! I know about the slander of those who say they are Jews and
are not, but are a synagogue of Satan. 10 Do not be afraid of what
you are about to suffer. I tell you, the devil will put some of you in
prison to test you, and you will suffer persecution for ten days. Be
faithful, even to the point of death, and I will give you life as your
victor's crown.11 Whoever has ears, let them hear what the Spirit

---

1. http://www.itstimetowakeupthetrees.com

says to the churches. The one who is victorious will not be hurt at all by the second death."Revelation 2:8 (Bible)

———

Smyrna

Sacral (Sacrum) chakra / energy centre

THE INNER FIRE

There are so many cross references to show the deeper meaning of the sacral energy from warnings of how this sexual energy, when perverted, can lead to death, and conversely to tantric union and bliss when the divine masculine meets the divine feminine.

Definitions: Jewish, Indian, Greek: The meaning of the name Smyrna is Myrrh: bitter.

The word myrrh corresponds with a common Semitic root m-r-r meaning "bitter," as in Aramaic ◇◇◇◇ murr and Arabic مُرّ murr. Known as the Balm of Gilead. Myrrh is gum resin from the Commiphora Gileadensis plant and has many uses, for example for embalming.

In the Greek Myth of Myrrha, she became bitter following an incestuous relationship with her father. Her son is Adonis, and she refused "acceptable / normal" forms of intercourse.

It is also known as The balm of Mecca. (Ref: 28)

Māra (◇◇◇).— m. the Evil One, the adversary and tempter One who tries to thwart the Bodhisattva or Buddha and his followers. Also known as Satan in Christian terms.

We can see through these definitions and translations the correlation between Smyrna/Myrhh and the sacral chakra, in that myrrh is known as the oil of joy and is given as an expensive gift of perfume, healing, embalming, or spiritual anointing oil either at a birth, a death, or a marriage.

In Isaiah 61:3 it says: "To give unto them beauty for ashes, the oil of joy for mourning, the garment of praise for the spirit of heaviness;

that they might be called trees of righteousness, the planting of the LORD, that he might be glorified." A very nice analogy.

The sacrum is the sacred place or Holy bone; the place where the masculine and feminine join as one through sexual union. It's the place where divine creation takes place, giving birth to new life. It's also our energy storage centre. It's where our inner fire is first ignited. Interestingly, the hidden meaning of Jesus/Jehoshua is fire. This is our inner fire: "I [Christ] am come to send fire on the earth..." (Luke 12:49). Jesus said, "I [Christ] have cast fire upon the world, and see, I am guarding it until it blazes." (Gospel of Thomas)

Comprehending the inner fire, its ignition and activation is key to full awakening. The Fornix inside the brain literally translates as furnace. It is part of the hippocampus and is said to ignite as internal ascension takes place. It also corresponds externally to the Fornax, a constellation of stars in the southern celestial hemisphere. This is a perfect example of as above so below. When the cerebral spinal fluid has been raised through each energy centre, it literally ignites the pineal and the foramen — translatable as For Amen. In the Bible it states that the Amen is Jesus. (Ref: 36)

The scripts tell us more about the holy fire:

".... He [Christ] shall baptize you with the Holy Spirit, and [with] fire: Whose fan [is] in his hand, and he will thoroughly purge his floor, and gather his wheat into the garner; but he will burn up the chaff with unquenchable fire." (Matthew 3:12, Luke 3:16)

It brings a whole new meaning to Pentecost and the tongues of fire. Think about it. Also, regardless of who or what inspired these scripts, perhaps it could be said that our inner fire is also there to consume the dross as well as act as a piezo electric circuit of energy. Fire purifies.

It has been said before that the Kundalini fire is the same thing as the Holy Spirit fire of Pentecost and the column of fire that led the Israelites out of Egypt. It is the Cosmic energy within us all, ignited through the internal process already expressed as raising the Chrism. There are myths surrounding this Kundalini process and a lot of nonsense that accompanies the sensations people have claimed to experience as a result of supposed activation. Some have opted for short-cuts, taking plant medicines and mind-bending drugs to have an awakening, albeit synthesised. An example of this forced growth and acceleration would be taking a flower bud just before it's about to bloom and ripping its petals open whilst shouting "grow!"

Swami Sivananda, age 124, the oldest man alive (that we know about) and also a doctor, speaks of his personal Kundalini activation: "Super-sensual visions appear before the mental eye of the aspirant, new worlds with indescribable wonders and charms unfold themselves before the Yogi, planes after planes reveal their existence and grandeur to the practitioner and the Yogi gets divine knowledge, power and bliss, in increasing degrees, when Kundalini passes through chakra after chakra, making them to bloom in all their glory which before the touch of Kundalini, do not give out their powers, emanating their divine light and fragrance and reveal the divine secrets and phenomena, which lie concealed from the eyes of worldly-minded people who would refuse to even believe of their existence."

Please take some time to watch the video regarding the Christ oil. Please note, the man who made the video has changed a lot over the years and I do not recommend his latter work. (Ref: 30) In my view, the Kundalini, the cerebral spinal fluid, and the Christ oil are one and the same thing. This thought will irk most Christians who consider the word Kundalini to be evil, let alone the natural

force of   energy. A hundred years ago I would have been burnt at the stake (again) for making this claim.

Women in the Bible

Another use of Myrrh is found in the chapter of Ester 2:12 (Bible) Interestingly, there are no accepted Biblical books written by women, only books about them. The book of Ester was written by Mordecai. The Nag Hammadi Scrolls revealed the Gospel of the Magdalene but it has never been accepted by the patriarchy.

"Each young woman's turn came to go into King Ahasuerus after she had completed twelve months' preparation, according to the regulations for the women, for thus were the days of their preparation apportioned: six months with oil of myrrh, and six months with perfumes and preparations for beautifying women." (I wonder what the King did to prepare himself?)

To be intimate with the King, Esther bathed in myrrh for six months and prepared another six with perfumes and cosmetics. It could be said that this symbolises the first initiation of the sacral energy centre. Being sexually prepared before meeting the king, or symbolically, the divine masculine, is something that Western cultures have lost. It is still part of some African traditions but is gradually being omitted by the current narrative for both boys and girls. The initiation into man and woman hood is a sacred, beautiful work. Now, it seems that the so-called controllers have removed the true definition of woman from the Cambridge English dictionary and replaced it with: "an adult[2] who lives[3] and identifies[4] as female[5] though they may have been said to have a different sex[6] at birth[7]" (Ref: 39)

This is another lie.

Our sacral centre develops from the age of eight and becomes active during puberty in readiness for procreation. When two people make love, the energy from their sex chakras mix and people who really love each other create an incredible aura around

---

2. https://dictionary.cambridge.org/dictionary/english/adult

3. https://dictionary.cambridge.org/dictionary/english/lives

4. https://dictionary.cambridge.org/dictionary/english/identify

5. https://dictionary.cambridge.org/dictionary/english/female

6. https://dictionary.cambridge.org/dictionary/english/sex

7. https://dictionary.cambridge.org/dictionary/english/birth

themselves. — If we question what the aura is, it's an electrical charge. The inner fire ignites and is manifested on all levels. Wilhelm Reich used to call this energy orgone and postulated it in the 1930s.

Awakening the sacral chakra can have strong positive and negative effects, as the energy is powerful. It's like fire walking. Just think about the power it takes to create another person. It's so incredible, beautiful, and raw. Childbirth is no walk in the park, and as a mother, I know from experience!

From the negative perspective, I am once again taken to the Greek myth of Myrrha, who became bitter following intercourse with her father. After giving birth to her son Adonis, she refused "acceptable forms" of intercourse (makes one wonder...).

Upon awakening this sacral energy, if not handled with care, it can lead to depravity, lust, and perversion. Perhaps this is because of a lack of knowledge regarding energy itself? It's like a rip tide carrying the unaware person away; the sacral energy is so powerful that if not channelled well, it can create feedback, or an energy vortex, rather like a consuming whirlpool in effect. It's my belief that in the future, all superstition will be replaced by the supernatural and spiritual and scientific comprehension of what and who we are and how universal energies react. In my dreams I have seen the equivalent of a spiritual periodic table with quantum and multi-dimensional elements that are beyond our current generic knowledge. It is almost like quantum alchemy.

Let's continue with more from John's church of Ephesus.

"I know about the slander of those who say they are Jews and are not, but are a synagogue of Satan..." Revelation 2:9 (Ref: 37)

To explain this quote, I am taken to the Talmud, which is very different from the Mosaic Law (Ten Commandments). One of the things the Talmud allows is paedophilia, among other debauched things (Ref: 29). There are plenty of references to this should you wish to check them out.

There's much controversy regarding the true meaning of the word Jew. It's best to do your own research in this case. My opinion is that to be Jewish means to be born of the land of Judea, which would include all the tribes living in that area. Once again, opposing religious traditions and controlled factions cause endless problems regarding this matter. Plus, ça change?

Metaphorically speaking, this is all about betrayal, perversion, and mis-use of this energy centre, illustrated by the script in Revelation chapter two of the Bible.

"10 Do not be afraid of what you are about to suffer. I tell you; the devil will put some of you in prison to test you, and you will suffer persecution for ten days. Be faithful, even to the point of death, and I will give you life as your victor's crown." (Ref: 38)

It could be said that this is a warning to say that as the inner fire rises, the Kundalini or Christ oil purifies every centre. If one uses self-discipline, restraint, and remains faithful throughout the temptations, which always come during the purification process, the energy will rise, open the crown chakra, creating the Divine channel to source and the Victor's Crown will be worn.

Some people create fake enlightenment by using mushrooms, peyote, ayahuasca, or LSD. As previously stated, why force a natural process? Resisting the temptation to lose self-control is of great spiritual benefit. Allow the process to happen naturally, and just like the seasons or the life cycle of a tree, we might find that allowing nature to take her course is preferable.

It could also be said that Jesus took on the role of the anointed one following his forty-day fast in the desert. This could be taken both literally and allegorically. I believe Jesus' awakening happened on all levels of consciousness, from the physical to the spiritual, resulting in the opening of all energy centres. Jesus, the man, (it is said) was a great healer, a sage, a rebel, and a selfless individual. That is what Christ consciousness is; it exists on every level, in each and every man and woman as an oil, a frequency, and an energy.

Pain:

We're all tested and sometimes it hurts, a lot. However, pain serves to wake us up from our unconsciousness or spiritual slumber. As the Christ dwells within us, each part of us is cleansed through forgiveness, true unconditional love, and honouring the Creator. The Christ will cleanse each centre and detach us from the wheel of karma, fate, or cause and effect because if it doesn't, why pray? Why pray if we can't change things? We can. We can, through the power of love (Christ), change into our best selves. We can create our reality through the inner consciousness and Divine connection.

To again quote Steve Lecaz, scientist/engineer: "Again, it can be no coincidence that herein lies the largest Energy quasi-electrical store of the body, at the lowest impedance possible because of its proximity to, and thus ability to act as the principle drivers of the body (i.e. the legs) without energy loss."

This beautiful design is so beyond our comprehension regardless of what the people of the so-called elite profess. They may try to emulate the circuitry (i.e. via A.I.), but their arrogance will trip them up every time. The God-design is made with such love and compassion that the counterfeit will fall at the first hurdle, destroying itself and others.

If you are someone who does not subscribe to a single creator (or creators), just take a deeper look at our DNA and all that issues from it. Acknowledging there is a higher intelligence or consciousness (even if that is ourselves in another dimension or a collective or the Sun or God or Jesus or the Holy Spirit or whatever you wish to call it) is the key to opening the door to the infinite.

In human form, we can only copy the infinite and learn to expand our awareness as we go. We are like little children learning to walk. Think about it, in order to create universes and solar systems, we

have to graduate the playground.

Pergamos—Solar   Plexus   Energy   Centre.

Once again, we see a triangle pointing south to earth as symbolised in electronics.

———

THE SOLAR PLEXUS IS also known in Vedic tradition as Manipura (Sanskrit: ◇◇◇◇◇◇,) and is the third primary chakra. In the centre of the symbol we see the Sanskrit word "Ram." One of the most powerful primary chakras. Why? Because we receive and release energy into our bio-fields at this centre. It can also be taken or stolen from this place by others. This energy centre is like our own personal sun (sol=sun) and is used to manifest our soul's purpose here on this plane. How many times have you felt excitement or dread or any other visceral emotion in this area? Where does our energy come from? From the Sun. (Jesus = the sun of God). N.B.: The derivation of the word visceral is viscera which are the organs in the cavities of the body, especially those in the abdominal cavity. This directly relates to the area of the Solar Plexus and illustrates how much the language of our bodies is translated into words and form.

Along with each chakra, there is a sonic resonance, a sound frequency relevant to each organ and area of the body, mind, etheric body, and spirit. It's my belief that we naturally know what these sounds are when we allow our minds to quieten and our spirit to speak. We all have our own resonant frequency and, in fact, our own UNIQUE blood-song. (Ref: 25) Imagine that every angle creates a resonance and apply this to our bodies. There is nobody like you. You are a new creation.

To illustrate the blood-song, I am taken to the chapter of Hebrews 12:24 in the Bible:

"And to Jesus the mediator of the new covenant, and to the blood of sprinkling, that speaketh better things than that of Abel."

The meaning, we are generically told, is that Jesus' blood speaks a better word. But what does this really mean?

Firstly, Abel, when translated from Hebrew, means vanity or to be vain. Jesus, we know is related to all sorts of names from Zeus to anointed one or salvation. As we join the dots together, we can see that the resonance of the blood and DNA is the key to raising our own vibration and, if all is frequency from intentions, words, feelings, and thoughts to the rhythm of our heart beats (literally everything), then we had better take full responsibility for all that we are in this moment, all we have become, and all we truly are infinitely. Knowing these things surely empowers us to transcend (or as my friend Sylvia put it: TRANCE END) into our best version of ourselves and align with our Creator and the Christ energy or Light within us.

Knowing that all is frequency, we know that DISSonance creates DIS-ease. The key to unlock the power to heal ourselves and each other are the frequencies of forgiveness, compassion, unconditional love. These are all the good things we know about, but perhaps find hard to use when we have been given what looks like a rough road to travel. When we take the words of Jesus only, we see that the Christ seed is pure love. That doesn't mean doormat or fool. According to the scripts, Jesus the man was feisty and highly disciplined. However, He was also the embodiment of compassion, wisdom, and truth. I am grateful for this plumb-line in my life... and God knows I need it!

What is the meaning of Pergamos and why has this word been used to describe the Solar Plexus?

In Doctor Jerry Tennant's book *Healing is Voltage* we learn that the body is set up very much like a battery. Just like with a battery, when it's run completely dry, the poles shift from positive to negative. In order for healing to occur, the cells need to be running at over minus fifty millivolts. Please bear this in mind when reading the following correlating how energy has been personified as good and bad. In order to tell children about a complicated bit of science, the teacher occasionally opts for the personification of the elements involved to illustrate and animate its function. It could be said that this process has been used upon the masses and has got completely out of hand, hence people becoming religious and worshiping a statue instead of realising the truth of what it symbolises.

Buddhists worshiping Buddha (he would turn in his grave), Christians worshiping Jesus, Moslems worshiping a black box, and

Satanists worshiping the form of the Devil. Forgive me for being so blunt but what on Earth are they thinking?

NB: The etymology of Satan is SATURN.

> **The seat of satan**
>
> Jesus submits that Pergamum was host to "satan's throne" and "dwelling place" (2:13), but it should be noted that both Smyrna and Philadelphia housed a "synagogue of satan" (2:9, 3:9) and that at Thyatira folks went after the "deep things of satan" (2:24).

The world's elite worship Saturn. In the same way that Christianity has been codified in symbols and parables, so has the demonic cult of Saturnism. To de-mystify this area means going into muddy waters. As someone who loves the Christ consciousness, I pray to be like the lotus, allowing nothing to stick as I research this subject.   Here   goes:

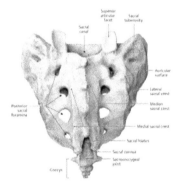

Pergamos is known as the seat of Satan. In Hindu tradition this is parallel to Shiva, the God of destruction. Bear in mind that we are also talking about the physical parts of the body, as well as its energy systems, positive and negative current and voltage.

The seat of Saturn is situated within our body. Firstly, let's remove any demonisation and superstition.

We can clearly see that the shape of Satan is at the ROOT, as seen in the image. It is easy to see how it has been personified. So, what and who on Earth started to demonise it? It's a part of the skeletal system and such a beautiful design. It appears that true knowledge has been lost in translation opening the door to grave misinterpretation, superstition, and fear. If we see this part of the body for what it is and as the miraculous seat of wisdom and power upon which everything else is supported, it changes everything.

The Planet Saturn and its resonant frequency (like te Schumann resonance of the Earth) connects to parts of our body, as do all the planets and constellations. They are us and we are them. They are IN us and we are IN them. Each planet has a resonance, which is reflected in us, our organs, and our energy centres.

Jesus of Nazareth, on the other hand, teaches that all individuals are to partake in the anointment (2 CORINTHIANS 1:21, 1 JOHN 2:20), that all individuals therefore are to be Christs and Messiahs (that is: kings and priests), with no earthly superiors and with a direct link of communication with the Creator. In Christ, our orders come from within, like DNA.

In Vedic tradition, Saturn is connected to the root chakra—which would explain "the seat of Satan." To demonise this energy is ill informed. Saturnic energy is perceived as evil and pain-inflicting. It is noticeable that the anatomy above the heart is anatomically reflected below. The glottis and vocal cords are mirrored in the sexual organs, which is interesting as the birth canal is the passage for human form and the trachea and speech organs create form through sound.

Actually, Saturn is all about the realisation of inner truth and spiritual revelations. This might manifest through expedient means, but ultimately, it is all for our growth and spiritual expansion, no matter how hard it appears to be. An example of this would be those born in the mid 1960s, who all have Saturn in Pisces. They are spiritual seekers and have probably been through the fire. Saturn is like a spiritual Dad energy that wants to know exactly what is going on all the time. But fear not, this is all for our greater, long-term good. Take no notice of the rubbish that issues from those who would demonise the entire process.

The Black Box or Cube:

Jewish Rabbis wear black cubes on their foreheads. Moslems walk around a massive black cube in Mecca. The black cube is the symbol used by Satanists universally. Interesting.

A cube folds out into a cross. (Ref 40.1)

A cross represents many things, but one of them is a tesseract. Note Salvador Dali's crucifixion.

The tesseract is a fourth- and fifth-dimensional shape that correlates with the symbol of the cross. The spiritual process that happens within us once a month where the cerebral spinal fluid crosses the vagus nerve reflects that ascension. We are multidimensional beings and what happens to us has an effect in all dimensions and vice versa.

So let's dump the demonisation and comprehend the energies of positive and negative electricity within us and externally.

―――――――

SOLAR PLEXUS:

Look carefully and you will see the personification in the images below.

Remember, our blood from the outside appears to be blue INSIDE our body in the veins. The blue appearance of Shiva symbolises the INSIDE of our body—our veins or venous system.

Definitions: The Solar Plexus is a large plexus of sympathetic nerves in the abdomen behind the stomach (plexus: a network, as of nerves or blood vessels. Any complex structure containing an intricate network of parts.) (Ref: 40, 40.1

Solar plexus: (Anat.) a nervous plexus situated in the dorsal and anterior part of the abdomen, consisting of several sympathetic ganglia with connecting and radiating nerve fibres — so-called in allusion to the radiating nerve fibres.

The Solar (Sun) Plexus (a structure in the form of a network, especially of nerves, blood vessels, or lymphatics) is also known as the celiac plexus.

Celiac — House of bread — Bethlehem Please see Ref 40.1

(Images from the complete anatomy app.)

One does not have to use much imagination to see how all language is naturally connected to the body, each neurone, synapse, every dendritic circuit and flow, each electrical impulses and current is mirrored in the glyphs and symbols we string together.

What if we are more naturally inteligent than we consciously know? What if every external letter symbolises a part of the body? What if every part of the innerverse is found in the outerverse, our beautiful strucures emmanating into the quantum field in dimensions and sacred geometric resonances our minds can comprehend, reconciling itself to itself infinitely?

By truly perceiving the connectedness of all things, our respect for all life increases along with our capacity for peace, freedom, joy, wisdom, compassion and innerstanding.

The Language of our Body:

The solar plexus nerves, as one can see from the short video in Ref40.1, look like symbolic language. When I saw this for the first time, something deep inside my being resonated.

"The seed is the word and the word is the seed and the word is the beginning." (Ref: 41) Please apply this to the postulate regarding the language of the body.

The Seed:

The Christ seed is born in the Bethlehem or coeliac plexus / solar (sun / son) plexus. Christ the "sun" or "son" of God. How beautiful to describe it this way; how foolish to take it so literally from scripture.

The disconnection and demonisation of the human body is such a terrible thing. It is essential for us to honour who and what we are. What a marvel. What a creation!

When we start to unpick the symbols, the language, and the anatomy of each part, it gets more and more interesting. What an incredible work of art. I stand in awe.

How the Solar Plexus correlates to the solar system internally and externally, the Lunisolar calendar, all languages interrelate, how the internal and external reality correlates is all such a beautiful symphony of light and sound, infinitely playing its song of creation and life, awaiting our acknowledgement. (Ref: 42)

I'm no biologist, but it is easy to see that the scripts have symbolised what and who we are.

I've only scratched the surface and I feel sure there are many who have made better connections than I have. However, I hope that I have inspired new thoughts and realisations.

The Inner Sky

"MARVEL NOT IF WE SAY that these are within thee but understand that thou thyself art another world in little, and hast within thee the sun and the moon, and also the stars." (Ref: 43)

Steve Lecaz describes this from an electrical and energetic perspective: "So the solar plexus from an electrical standpoint can be seen as the power station from which the body derives all energies it needs to thrive. The calorific values of foods is translated into muscle power to drive limbs and the heart and to supply the brain with the nutrients it requires. As we move up the body, the electrically low impedance rises, moving largely from high current physical demand upwards through to ever higher impedance and lower current cerebral activities. It should be noted that higher impedance paths are more capable at working at higher frequencies."

This correlates perfectly with music and sound and light. A symphony of life, played by our own consciousness, danced by our bodies, and sung into being through the power of our own voice.

Thyatira—The Heart chakra

Greek definition: White Castle.

"THE 'WHITE CASTLE' is a symbol of achievement, of destiny perfectly fulfilled and of spiritual perfection. Between the black and the white, at intervals, stand the other castles of the soul described by the mystics, as successive resting-places along the path of sanctification. The castle of illumination, on the mountain peak, merging with the sky itself, is where the soul will for ever be united with its God and will fully and mutually enjoy that untarnishable presence." (Ref: http://dreamicus.com/castle.html)

The castle of Thyatira (what's left of it) was once known as the church that condoned sin

What on Earth was meant comparing Thyatira to Jezebel and the condoning of sin?

Historically speaking, as far as I can see, this part of Revelation has been edited by the Catholic Church to remove the true meaning of what John was saying. Once again human intervention assures the population that the Divine feminine can be blamed for leading people astray into sin and for generating all the misdeeds the population carried out. How convenient.

Let's examine the Hebrew definition: A perfume, sacrifice of labour. A labour of love. The ultimate sacrifice. Unconditional love.

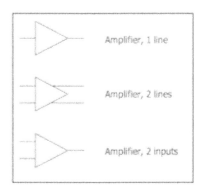

IN THE ABOVE PICTURE of the heart chakra, we see two triangles and the Sanskrit letter A in the centre. Firstly, let us look at this from a scientific perspective. One triangle points to earth (remember the electrical symbol for earth) the other to the sky, and this, it could be said, correlates with the electrical symbol for an antenna.

It is the place in the body where the energies meet, like a big junction box. It creates the well-known star shape associated with so many things, including Solomon's seal. (Sol=sun. Om = Ohm. On = [city of] light). (Ref: 44)

As a voice specialist, I noticed many years ago (as previously mentioned) that all that is above the heart is reflected below it. It's as if the heart operates as the fulcrum of our own inner reflection, acting like a physical mirror. The brain looks like the intestine, the jaw looks like the hips, the vocal cords and glottis look like the vulva and the tongue speaks life (or death) just as the womb creates life. It is all exquisitely designed and falls into the old adage: "As above so below." The energy meets at the heart and the heart itself is the main junction box of the body.

There is a lot to say about the heart. In fact, a whole book could be written on this area alone, so I will try to condense the data into salient points so you can make that journey yourself should you wish. My next book will be a journey of the heart.

· Our heartbeats synchronise when we sing together;

· One cell from the heart split into two pieces will beat in sync with the other no matter where it is in the universe;

· Our hearts become physically scarred — even lacerated — when we go through trauma;

· The geometry of the heart creates its resonance which, on the whole, is around 528 Hertz. It's the shape of the heart or the space within it that creates the resonance.

Energy flowing toward the Earth, as reflected in this symbol:

ENERGY FLOWING TOWARD the Sky, as reflected in this image:

TOGETHER THE TWO TRIANGLES create the well-known symbol:

"AND IT CAME ABOUT THROUGH my prayer that grace was given to me from the Lord Sabaoth by Michael his archangel. [He brought me] a little ring, having a seal consisting of an engraved stone, and said to me: "Take, O Solomon, king, son of David, the gift which the Lord God has sent thee, the highest Sabaoth. With it thou shalt lock up all demons of the earth, male and female; and with their help thou shalt build up Jerusalem. [But] thou [must] wear this seal of God. And this engraving of the seal of the ring sent thee is a Pentalpha." (Ref: 45)

Sol—Sun, Om—Ohm, On—city of light Heliopolis

It is important to note that King Solomon's testimony is an esoteric, magical work said to have first been written in Greek. Please apply critical thinking and modern science to this allegory.

The comparison between the people of Thyatira and the heart chakra resonates with the Hebrew translation: a perfume or sacrifice of labour. Historically speaking, Thyatira was known for its trade guilds including wool, linen, baking, leather, bronze, famous purple dyes, and unfortunately, slaves. They were hard-working people who apparently were mostly Turkish Jewish converts. As a result, there was a real mixture of spiritual practices going on from Paganism, Human sacrifice, Judaism, and early Christianity.

The heart is where the energy from the Earth (negative) meets the energy from the Sun (positive) and creates the six-pointed star we all know so well. The symbol is a simplification and slightly two dimensional, however, the words of the scripture describe the positive and negative energies we feel so deeply in the heart.

Personally, I think we have moved on from this simplification and have innerstood the true energy of the Heart: Unconditional love, selflessness, and compassion. More about that in later chapters.

SARDIS OR 'SARDIUS' – Throat chakra

SARD IS ONE OF THE stones found in the Jewish Ephod. A couple of interesting things here:

The twelve tribes of Judah are actually symbolic of the twelve signs of the Zodiac mirrored in the 12 cranial nerves and the 12 apostles.

The Ephod looks a lot like technology to either build some sort of radio or to protect oneself from particular frequencies. Notice the eye symbol at the top of the ephod. This represents the inner eye, the pineal gland, or as some call it, the all-seeing eye of God. You will find this symbol on the Dollar Bill, in Masonic Temples, in Greece, and in Turkey worn to protect from evil. In fact, some see it as the Ark of the Covenant itself.

There are many things that could be said about the external representation of The Ark of the Covenant from myths and legends told in the Bible and other scripts to the Indiana Jones Hollywood special effects unit creating a fearful sonic transmitter and receiver, a sort of weaponised, dangerous, direct communication line to God.

However, at this point, we have arrived at the throat chakra and the correlation between Sard, Sardius, and Sardis. Please go to Ref: 45.1. I am sure you will see the visual correlation to the thyroid.

> The stone Sardis is also known as Carnelian, a variant of Chalcedony. This stone was first discovered in Greece, in Sardis. The old Hebrew name for this was Odem. (Ref: 46)

As you can see, the stones look very similar in colour and texture to the thyroid gland, which of course, is situated right in the middle of the throat.

"And unto the angel of the church in Sardis write; These things saith he that hath the seven Spirits of God, and the seven stars; I know thy works, that thou hast a name that thou livest, and art dead."4 Thou hast a few names even in Sardis which have not defiled their garments; and they shall walk with me in white: for they are worthy. 5 He that overcometh, the same shall be clothed in white raiment; and I will not blot out his name out of the book of life, but I will confess his name before my Father, and before his angels.6 He that hath an ear, let him hear what the Spirit saith unto the churches. (Ref. Revelation 47:3)

The thyroid gland is situated just below the Adam's Apple (more about that one later) and its functions include maintaining:

· Regular breath

· Heart rate

· Body weight

· Muscle strength

· Menstrual cycles

· Body temperature

· Cholesterol levels

· Metabolic rate

· Digestive function

· Bone maintenance

· Brain development

Research states that the thyroid is very sensitive and prone to imbalance. The hormones T3 and T4 that the thyroid creates can be easily upset but, by what? By the mind and the little rudder that steers the body called the tongue. We speak our intentions into this dimension and bring them into manifestation through repetition. We know that whatever we focus our attention on becomes our reality both internally and externally. We also know that modes of thinking are inherited unless we change the inner dialogue.

In the scripture from Revelation chapter three above, it asks you to hold fast, repent, and overcome. Through the process of revelation and realisation, if we stand still, hold fast amidst the storm, we can overcome our lower nature. We can change our mental frequency and refrain from cursing with our tongues. (Can salt water and pure water come from the same spring?)

In verse 4 it says:

"Thou hast a few names even in Sardis which have not defiled their garments; and they shall walk with me in white: for they are worthy." (Ref: 47)

Defiling one's garment would mean defiling one's body, inner and outer. The rest is obvious.

The structure of the Sard/Chalcedony stone is of interest:

"Chalcedony is a cryptocrystalline form of silica, composed of very fine intergrowths of quartz and moganite." (Ref: 48)

This stone can also be blue (as well as red, green, black, white, yellow, pink, etc.), which is the more common colour for the throat chakra. It has a hexagonal structure. The healing properties of the stone are numerous.

Interestingly, thyroid hormones also have a crystalline structure:

I postulate that what was actually being said in Revelation three (without reading too much into it) was that our intentions either uplift us or defile us. Applying this to the throat energy centre will either create life or death through the intention spoken into being on this plane. Intention itself has frequency and vibration and the words are the sonic latent effect. The following scripture illustrates this point:

"The tongue has the power of life and death, and those who love it will eat its fruit." (Ref: 50)

Philadelphia—Third eye/pineal chakra

"7 And to the angel of the church in Philadelphia write; These things saith he that is holy, he that is true, he that hath the key of David, he that openeth, and no man shutteth; and shutteth, and no man openeth;8 I know thy works: behold, I have set before thee an open door, and no man can shut it: for thou hast a little strength, and hast kept my word, and hast not denied my name.9 Behold, I will make them of the synagogue of Satan, which say they are Jews, and are not, but do lie; behold, I will make them to come and worship before thy feet, and to know that I have loved thee.10 Because thou hast kept the word of my patience, I also will keep thee from the hour of temptation, which shall come upon all the world, to try them that dwell upon the earth.11 Behold, I come quickly: hold that fast which thou hast, that no man take thy crown.12 Him that overcometh will I make a pillar in the temple of my God, and he shall go no more out: and I will write upon him the name of my God, and the name of the city of my God, which is new Jerusalem, which cometh down out of heaven from my God: and I will write upon him my new name.13 He that hath an ear, let him hear what the Spirit saith unto the churches." (Ref: 52)

Definitions: Philo- before vowels phil-, word-forming element meaning "loving, fond of, tending to," from Greek philos (adj.) "dear, loved, beloved" (Ref: 52)

Philadelphia — Also the name recalls that of the ancient city in Lydia, mentioned in the New Testament, which was so called in honour of Attalos II Philadelphos, 2c B.C.E. king of Pergamon, who founded it. His title is said to have meant "loving the brother (brethren)." (Ref: 53)

Adelphi — From Greek adelphos "brother," literally "from the same womb, co-uterine," from copulative prefix a- "together with" (see a- (3)) + delphys "womb," which is a word related to dolphin, which is interesting. (Ref: 54)

Dolphin (n.) — "Popular name of a diverse group of marine mammals, also including the porpoise (but the true dolphin has a longer and more slender snout), (Ref: 55) mid-14c., dolfin, from Old French daulphin, from Medieval Latin dolfinus, from Latin delphinus "dolphin," from Greek delphis (genitive delphinos) "dolphin," related to delphys womb. (Ref: 56) Popularly applied to The Dorado (which means dolphinfish) from late 16c. The constellation is so called from early 15c." (Ref: 57)

We see from Reference 55 that there is a dolphin shape in the brain known as the Third ventricle. Its function is to help produce and secrete the cerebral spinal fluid, protect the brain from trauma or injury, and to transport nutrients and waste from the body's central nervous system. I find it notable that The Dorado constellation is so named and if I had a good comprehension of astronomy, I would postulate that it correlates to the hemispheres of our brain. (Ref: 58)

There is so much to say about the third ventricle, the fornix, the pineal and pituitary glands that I will have to cover it all in another chapter. For now:

"7 And to the angel of the church in Philadelphia write; These things saith he that is holy, he that is true, he that hath the key of David, he that openeth, and no man shutteth; and shutteth, and no man openeth" (Ref: 59)

Let's translate:

And to the "angle" of the energy centre (church/temple) in the place of the beloved dolphin (third and fourth ventricle of the brain), he that has the opened the door (Biblically, key means opening) of love, (David means beloved and the man David had "the heart of God") of the heart, no man can shut or open.

Meaning that love is the only key to open the inner doorway.

No man can open or shut this door; only the frequency of love felt in the heart will ever unlock the inner and upper worlds. It could be said that "Love it the Key to Life." (I wrote a song about that.) The teaching of Christ is all about love. The words of Christ are to liberate ourselves through the power of Divine, unconditional love.

All the other stuff in the scriptures fades because ultimately, this universe is built on love. The outplaying of everything depends on how much Love there is in it.

If love is a frequency, then love has a key, in French: "clef." Both words are used to alternately represent the key to unlock doors and the musical tone.

We know that all is frequency and sound. We know that love has a key and a resonance. The geometric shape of a man or woman's heart creates a resonant frequency. That frequency varies somewhat but is around the key of B flat to C in most of us. When love is absent, there will be a discord or dis-chord / dis-accord or 'dis-sonance'. Chord means more than one note together — either harmonic or enharmonic. Accord means agreement; or the same thoughts about something; or it could be said: harmony.

We know that sound creates form (Ref: 60), so we can see that discord will never be able to create harmony or accord unless it resolves itself, just as it does in music, eventually coming back to the fundamental or "key" the original piece is played in.

Please see exactly where the pineal gland is in relation to the third and fourth ventricle of the brain. You can do this by going to Ref: 60.1

8 I know thy works: behold, I have set before thee an open door, and no man can shut it: for thou hast a little strength, and hast kept my word, and hast not denied my name. (Ref: 61)

The door is opened when the teachings of love are adhered to. In the most Holy Scripts, the teachings of universal love and compassion prevail. It's all about love. But who really knows what love is? We only know what it isn't.

"Most people are unhappy and they are unhappy because there is no love in their hearts." J. Krishnamurti (Ref: 62)

Energy

Energy is either positive or negative in duality. We get to choose which kind of energy we direct and how, however, when adverse intentions/energy is sent our way it can become stuck, hooked in, or knocks us for six, especially if it's unexpected. But it can only affect us if the sender is of equal strength. Staying in our Divine power is the key.

LAODICIA — CROWN CHAKRA

Translation: Place Of People Of Common Fairness

Also known as "Lod, the city of Zeus," otherwise known as "The city of God."

Om (Hindu symbol) or Ohm (Electrical unit of electrical resistance, transmitting a current of one ampere when subjected to a potential difference of one volt.) Represents:

· Divinity

· The spiritual self

· Unity and inter-connectivity of all things

· Oneness with the universe

In the biblical scripture Revelation chapter three verses fourteen to twenty-two it states:

14 "To the angel of the church in Laodicea write: These are the words of the Amen, the faithful and true witness, the ruler of God's creation. 15 I know your deeds, that you are neither cold nor hot. I wish you were either one or the other! 16 So, because you are lukewarm—neither hot nor cold—I am about to spit you out of my mouth. 17 You say, 'I am rich; I have acquired wealth and do not need a thing.' But you do not realize that you are wretched, pitiful, poor, blind and naked.

18 I counsel you to buy from me gold refined in the fire, so you can become rich; and white clothes to wear, so you can cover your shameful nakedness; and salve to put on your eyes, so you can

see.19 Those whom I love I rebuke and discipline. So be earnest and repent. 20 Here I am! I stand at the door and knock. If anyone hears my voice and opens the door, I will come in and eat with that person, and they with me.21 To the one who is victorious, I will give the right to sit with me on my throne, just as I was victorious and sat down with my Father on his throne. 22 Whoever has ears, let them hear what the Spirit says to the churches." (Ref: 63)

Definition of Amen: Ammon's horn (Ref: 64). The above quote states: "They are the words of the Amen." The Amen is Jesus and is joined to the hippocampus. The Ram's horn symbolises the same thing and is directly taken from the Kemetic tradition (Amun-Ra) and permeates many ancient symbols, art, and sculptures from Ancient Greece to the effigies of the green man in Druidic Britain. It seems that the Ancients knew so much more than we are conscious of. Here we are in this dimension in the twenty-first century externally disconnected from our true heritage We've been digitised and boxed in by a senseless narrative where men can identify as women, girls identify as boys as young as four years old, and where true science is made into fiction. (Image Reference 65)

The Merriam-Webster dictionary's definition and derivation of the word Hippocampus is:

"from Greek hippokampos seahorse, from hippos horse + kampos sea monster. A curved elongated ridge that extends over the floor of the descending horn of each lateral ventricle of the brain, that consists of gray matter covered on the ventricular surface with white matter, and that is involved in forming, storing, and processing memory" (Ref: 66)

Neurologists recognise the hippocampus as each of two elongated protruberances (called hippocampus major and minor) on the floor of each lateral ventricle of the brain. They also look like horns as well as the galloping front legs of a horse, as you will see in the last reference.

It could be said that the scripture means: "To the energy centre in the city of God (i.e. the crown), these are the words of the 'Amen' (issuing from the grey matter in the Ammon's horn) the true witness and the ruler of God's creation." The word "witness" alludes to consciousness or awareness. Ammon's horn is a part of the brain responsible for the higher mind, or consciousness, emotions, and memory. This memory is both long- and short-term, but I postulate it is also rather like what is known as the Akashic Record, the record of every thought, word, and deed that has ever happened. I postulate that it could be contained in our genetic memory as well as the infinite spiritual memory of lives on and off of this plane. I propose that just as batteries store excess energy in their electromagnetic fields, so do we. I postulate that memories and incidents are stored as energy (positive and negative) in the torus field. This would help to explain being able to work with tuning the human bio-field with sonic frequencies, bearing in mind that all is vibration and frequency including thoughts, emotions, and sound or spoken words. By tuning the energy centres and human electro-magnetic field, one can release trauma and blockages which cause DIS-ease in the mind, body, and spirit. (Ref: 66)

The Limbic System:

It should be more obvious to you as the reader where I am going with all of this. It seems to me that all so-called Holy books are all telling us the same things in different ways. They are all showing us the anatomy of the mind, body, and spirit and how to best function in this dimension. They describe everything from our physiology and states of consciousness, deep esoteric processes to the law of cause and effect, sometimes in an articulate way and at other times, primitively, humanistically, and vengefully, depending on the scribe. Ultimately, whether it is describing the twelve cranial nerves, amygdala, or the tree of life in parable form, the main thread that runs from beginning to end is that the strongest, most potent power in the universe is love. God is love.

Here is an explanation of the previous scripture "15 I know your deeds, that you are neither cold nor hot. I wish you were either one or the other! 16 So, because you are lukewarm—neither hot nor cold—I am about to spit you out of my mouth. 17 You say, 'I am rich; I have acquired wealth and do not need a thing.' But you do not realize that you are wretched, pitiful, poor, blind and naked." (Ref: 63)

It could be said that the above scripture alludes to the lack of energy and mental focus or emotional direction toward the spirit. The 'Ohm' is not functioning or flowing. Instead, the energy has been used for material gain, distractions, emotional dysfunction, and not for connecting to the Divine. (Ref: 67)

Continuing: "18 I counsel you to buy from me gold refined in the fire, so you can become rich; and white clothes to wear, so you can cover your shameful nakedness; and salve to put on your eyes, so you can see.19 Those whom I love I rebuke and discipline.

So be earnest and repent. 20 Here I am! I stand at the door and knock. If anyone hears my voice and opens the door, I will come in and eat with that person, and they with me.21 To the one who is victorious, I will give the right to sit with me on my throne, just as I was victorious and sat down with my Father on his throne. 22 Whoever has ears, let them hear what the Spirit says to the churches." (Reference 63)

In the above scripture, God is rebuking those who don't practice the deeper teachings of selfless love, purification, and the opening of the pineal and therefore the crown chakra. I find the words clumsy and poorly written and not the words one might expect from an all-seeing intelligence. If we are the spark of creator, then this passage seems to be a very humanistic approach to self-sabotage, and not too encouraging.

The scripture continues:

"I counsel you to buy from me gold refined in the fire, so you can become rich; and white clothes to wear, so you can cover your shameful nakedness; and salve to put on your eyes, so you can see." (Ref: 63)

It could be said that the "Gold refined in the fire" is the melatonin in the cerebral-spinal fluid, the Christ oil, refined through the crucifixion at the vagus nerve and potentised upon re-entry into the pineal, opening the inner door to the Godhead. The White clothes symbolise the "milky substance" that is created in the pituitary gland. These hormones are the known as "The Christ or Holy Oil."

"Shameful nakedness" means it's obvious to see what's happening in error. This reminds me of the so-called born again preachers and spiritual teachers who are professing enlightenment yet spend their earnings on million-dollar houses and cars for themselves, never really healing anyone, leading people into false beliefs, and shepherding them into their own powerlessness.

We are being asked to turn inward, knock on the inner door, and HUMBLY go in and there; we have communion with the Divine intelligence that permeates the all that is. There, in that place, we sit at the Godhead, the inner throne situated in the right hemisphere of the brain.

As Bill Donahue says: "There is an organ in your brain called the hippocampus. It is your point of restoration to the memory of your true self. Here is something special: Stedmans Medical Dictionary defines the hippocampus of the brain as, 'the medial margin (hem) of the corticle (outer), mantle (garment).' It is the hem of the garment, and it is within you, closer than your breath."

In Matthew 14:35-36 (Bible) it states:

"..And when the men of that place recognised Him, they sent out into all that surrounding region, brought to Him all who were sick, and begged Him that they might only touch the hem of His garment. And as many as touched it were made perfectly well. (Ref: 68)

This shows that the body, mind, and spirit, through the use of the Limbic system, can regenerate and be healed. (Ref: 69) For those who are already awakened, the process of getting there is through purification on every level. Resisting the lower nature and ascending to higher realms through unconditional love, just as it is written in many Holy Books.

Bill Donahue has worked tirelessly on this subject over the past thirty years. It appears that we have realised similar things though I only found him recently. His work is extensive and I am just beginning. I am most grateful for his research and hope to expand upon some of it as we enter a new era of awakening to who we truly are.

The truth is within all of us and none of us have its copyright.

The White Horse and the Ouroboros

———

My nine years of life at Catholic boarding school was dominated by the same question: "Who am I?"

I was admonished by the other kids for being too deep and questioning everything as well as being the scholarship kid with no money. My school uniform was replaced once from the age of seven to fifteen, which was fortunate as mini dresses were in by the time I left. The nuns kept their beady eyes on me, watching to see if I might put a foot wrong. Then, during a doctrine lesson, I revealed at fourteen that I thought the Book of Revelation was a journey to self-realisation; it was then that they asked me to become one of them. Of course, my mother went berserk, bought me a book about a nun who escaped a vicious enclosed order, and enrolled me into a free school where we all regularly smoked pot with the teachers during our naked bathing sessions. Yeah — slight contrast. It took a while to find myself after all of that.

At the convent (which was a little bit like Hogwarts) I spent most of my time hiding in the music room singing songs and playing the guitar. Music (and Jesus) was my saviour and John Denver filled up all my senses, Donovan and Bob Dylan allowed me to find my inner rebellion, and *The Eagles: Hotel California* echoed down the miserable, stark stone corridors, cheering up the sad faces of the statues of Mary killing a snake with her foot and St. Patrick with his shamrock sweep-over hair-do.

I wasn't really interested in Lady so-and-so's lavish dresses, how many horses Shaniqua's daddy had, or fabulous, expensive, hot vacations like the rest of my class — although I did long to go on the class skiing trip every year, but never managed it as my parents drank their wages. Holidays for me usually meant having to put up with shouting-drunk parents who were either working or in the pub. I would have to sit in the corner of the The Windjammer public house while they got drunk and flirted their way across the bar to the next whisky. I would be given one orange juice and told to "make it last." That was my life. It gave me a lot of time to think, as there were no books in the house and I wasn't encouraged to learn save by the elderly gent who rented the spare room of the family home. It was Billy Becket who told me about the Tartars, promissory notes, and measured the width of my hair with his special device, the name of which I can't recall. (It's all lasers now.) I shall always be grateful to him for caring for me. My parents didn't really see me unless I was of use to them. I was like an invisible child, unseen and not heard. I remember how they regularly got me out of bed late at night to recite a poem or two for their drunken dinner guests saying: "We're paying all this money to give you elocution lessons; the least you could do is recite a poem." So, I would, in my perfect Julie Andrews voice. It was excruciating, especially when the drunk guests would repeat a line and laugh, mimicking and mocking me. Yes, it was an interesting childhood. Interesting because the parents were never home and when they were, I wished they weren't. I spent a lot of time alone or in my best friend's house, who still is and always will be, my best and dearest friend. My dearest Ellen.

Life has been an incredible journey so far. Full of extreme highs and deep lows, abundance, opulence, wealth, poverty, gain, and loss, all leading to this moment when I can finally allow myself to sit down, take stock, and share everything I have learnt with you, the reader.

All these old memories have had their emotional charge removed as I have learnt not to recreate them in a negative way and so most negative cycles have stopped repeating for me. What's so wonderful is the realisation that it all comes from within, and that all that is within, is with out.

I have to say, I think my hippocampus has had a lot of use!

(Image below from 'Complete anatomy app')

There are many different symbols for the Hippocampus. At first, I

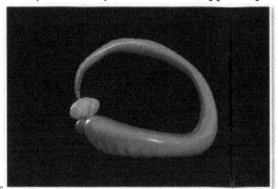

saw it as the snake eating its own tail. (Imagine, your hippocampus could be physically scarred from all the lifetimes of trauma. Wouldn't you want to heal that?)

So, what does this mean?

It means that whatever is going on inside our heads has a third or fourth dimensional representation in the physical realm.

THE HIPPOCAMPUS

(Image   below   from   The   Complete   Anatomy   app)

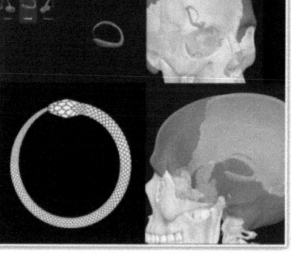

The Hippocampus, seahorse, White Horse, Ouroboros, Ram's Horn, Ammon's Horn, or Pegasus sits in the centre of the skull and, as previously stated, is responsible for long-term memories and much more. Just like any other organ in the body, it can become physically scarred if trauma is experienced as a result of carrying out a mental program on repeat. An example could be recreating the trauma as it's indented or branded onto the organic form.

The hippocampus is symbolised by the Ouroboros:

Definition: "Ouroboros: emblematic serpent of ancient Egypt and Greece represented with its tail in its mouth, continually devouring itself and being reborn from itself. A gnostic and alchemical symbol, Ouroboros expresses the unity of all things, material and spiritual, which never disappear but perpetually change form in an eternal cycle of destruction and re-creation." Ref: https://www.britannica.com/topic/Ouroboros

Plato thought that the Ouroboros was a perfect being in which everything resided.

The hippocampus was also known as Ammon's Horn. Ammon. Amen. Amun. Atum. Atom. Adam. Aten. Each of these words have been used over the centuries to mean the same thing and are derived mostly from Kemetic beliefs, i.e. Ancient Egyptian

philosophy.

"The term Ammon's horn is a metaphor that refers to the ram shaped horns on the head representing the Egyptian God Amun who protected the Pharaoh Taharqa in the temple of Kawa. Many temples were dedicated to Amun. The Greek form of the name was Ammon, the Libyan Jupiter whom the Greeks identified with Zeus. King David conquered a Jordanian tribe, the Ammonites, who were descendants of Lot, by the son of his younger daughter.

"It is of interest that the related hippocampal commissure together with the crura of the fornix, is sometimes termed the "psalterium" or "lyra Davidis". Psalterium and Lyra are both harps. To add to the confusion, French neuroanatomists refer to the horn-shaped lateral part of the fourth ventricle with its choroid plexus leaving the foramen like a posy of flowers as the "corne d'abondance" (horn

of plenty, or cornucopia)."   (Ref: 71)

Notice the shape of the Ammonite fossil, also known as a Snakestone.

Ammonites in the Bible were a Semitic people related to the Israelites. This can be taken allegorically too. Lot fathered the Ammonites in Sodom. (You might want to pause for a moment to contemplate that.)

"The Ammonites, descendants of Ben-Ammi, were a nomadic people who lived in the territory of modern-day Jordan, and the name of the capital city, Amman, reflects the name of those ancient inhabitants."

When God destroyed Sodom and Gomorrah, Lot and his daughters fled to the mountains and his daughters had an incestuous relationship with their father, giving birth to the Moabites. (Consider what might have happened in the internal worlds, and how this played out.)

That which is in us is manifests in the external world.

NB: The Semitic people use the Shofar to invoke the Divine. The Shofar is a Ram's Horn. Ammon's Horn. Here is the external representation of the inner world. Beautiful.

Why   use   a   Ram's   horn   to   call   upon   God?

Once again, the meaning of the symbols has been lost, misinterpreted, misused, is misleading, or is demonised. We need to consider the meaning of sound as a carrier wave for intention and consciousness at this point.

"The sound of the Shofar awakens our desire to become closer to God, a yearning for meaning and fulfilment, and reminds us of the ram slaughtered by our father Abraham in a test from God to demonstrate his loyalty and commitment. And yet all of these are only earthly explanations for a Divine Commandment." Ref: 72)

NB: The internal is manifested externally and vice versa. If one thinks about it, it could be said that if you lose your memories, you lose a big chunk of consciousness in the third dimension.

One of the functions of the hippocampus is to establish long-term memory and to create new ones. Having a damaged hippocampus can create big cognitive problems. But like with all parts of the body, scars can be healed. In fact, if you think about it, memories give us the abilities to cognise, compare, and differentiate, bringing about a greater awareness. The last thing we want to do is lose it or get stuck in a loop of repetitive patterning.

With all the energetic chaos in the world these days, it takes a concerted daily cleanse to keep our vibrations clear and high. Taking care of our instruments is key to safe travel throughout the multiverse.

The hippocampus is the Amen, Jesus, the Atom the "and so it is," the revelation of inner consciousness. The is within us. There is an abundance of metaphors available for this critical function: Horn of plenty, creator of abundance, the sound of the infinite Hum, the Om, and the universal vibrational field.

Don't be fooled by the lower vibrational agenda. Don't misread the signs. Don't be afraid of questioning the infinite within you.

"Ask and you shall receive. Seek and you SHALL find. Knock, and the door shall be opened." (Ref: 73)

The truth is hiding in plain sight for those who have eyes to see and ears to hear.

The revelations of all that is in scripture (the scripts) and the inner and outer worlds have been so mind-blowing on a personal level that it sometimes takes time to process the words into three dimensions. Taking something from a higher sphere and squashing it into a sentence can be challenging, hence the use of symbols and stories. This helps so that in some way we can innerstand; thus, we follow the ancient method.

One of my purposes here on this plane is to bring these things, these treasures of darkness, into the light without any religious restrictions or new age twaddle. It is up to you what you do with the knowledge.

I've recently angered many Christians who have been indoctrinated into the current belief system. My intention is not to enrage, especially as my love for Christ is what brought me to this point in the first place. Never mind, they are free to be where they are.

A few years ago, I was guided to question the symbol of the white horse. It started in scripture.

11 Now I saw heaven opened, and behold, a white horse. And He who sat on him was called Faithful and True, and in righteousness He judges and makes war. 12 His eyes were like a flame of fire, and on His head were many crowns. He [a]had a name written that no one knew except Himself. 13 He was clothed with a robe dipped in blood, and His name is called The Word of God. 14 And the armies in heaven, clothed in [b]fine linen, white and clean, **followed Him on white horses.** 15 Now out of His mouth goes a [c]sharp sword, that with it He should strike the nations. And He Himself will rule them with a rod of iron. He Himself treads the winepress of the fierceness and wrath of Almighty God. 16 And He has on His robe and on His thigh a name written: KING OF KINGS AND LORD OF LORDS. (Ref: 74 and 74.1 for the images)

This script is symbolic of the awakening that happens when the Christ is internally activated following internal crucifixion — i.e. when the cerebral spinal fluid returns to the pineal gland, potentised after 2.5 days in the tomb or claustrum. It is the moment of conscious awakening when the voltage is strong enough to blow the stone of the tomb (the fornix) away.

I allowed my mind to drift in contemplation and found myself in Westbury in the UK. I chuckled as I remembered a few years ago how some hippies turned it into a unicorn with a rather large member. Amusing. And there are more chalk horses all over the UK, the oldest is the Uffington White Horse, in Oxfordshire on

the Berkshire Downs near the Ridgeway.

I WAS REMINDED OF THE Ark of the Covenant and the angel wings pointed inward—toward the cerebrum. Then I got it.

The Horse is the Hippocampus, and the wings are the cerebrum or cherubim.

I thought about these horses back in 2018 and wondered what they symbolised. Then, it clicked: of course, it is the hippocampus. I then started to get images of Pegasus and on I drifted into the world of symbols. Hmmm... a horse with wings.

I am amazed at the way things have been so artistically anthropomorphised. The beauty of truth displayed in art communicates the depths of the unfathomable. Creation itself is beyond comprehension.

The arrows in the picture (Ref: 75) point to the wings, which could certainly symbolize the wings of Pegasus.

"He placed the cherubim inside the innermost room of the temple, with their wings spread out. The wing of one cherub touched one wall, while the wing of the other touched the other wall, and their wings touched each other in the middle of the room." (Ref: 76)

It all fits so beautifully together. The walls are the skull. The Cherubim are the cerebrum, their heads are the centre of the brain, the pineal.

"The hippocampus is a limbic system structure that is precisely connecting emotions and senses, such as smell and sound, to memories. The hippocampus is an arching band of nerve fibers (fornix) combining the hippocampal formations in the left and right brain hemispheres look like a horseshoe-shaped structure. The hippocampus is located in the brain's, inner medial region of temporal lobes and works as a memory indexer by transferring memories out to the relevant part of the cerebral hemisphere for the long-term storehouse and retrieving them when necessary. It is also deemed to play an influential role in spatial processing and navigation." (Ref: 77)

In the Bible, it states that the woman with the issue of blood was healed through touching the hem of Jesus' garment. (Ref: 68)

Amygdala

"The amygdalae interpret external stimuli like sights and sounds as potentially dangerous and send that information to the hippocampus. This process activates a release of energy so you can respond to and protect yourself from external threats (the flight-or-fight response).1 The amygdalae are also responsible for assigning values to moments and turning them into memories." (Ref: 78) So we can deduce that the Hippocampus is an extremely important piece of kit. In fact, it is the instrument used for neurogenesis. The amygdalae are the two ends of the hippocampus and look like the hooves of a galloping horse.

I postulate that the release of energy (as aforementioned) is the energy ascending through the chakras and the voltage is dependent on the clarity and function of each energy centre. The Fornix is the vault or volt, which is where the energy ascends to and ignites, rolling the stone of the "tomb" away to create ascension and complete enlightenment.

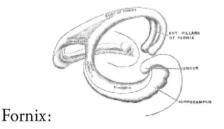

Fornix:

———————————

THE FORNIX IS THE ARCHED part of the top of Ammon's Horn.

This is another example of how the outer world is also the inner world.

Firstly, Bill Donahue explains what this is very nicely in his video number 584 "The Biblical Temple is the Brain".

The interior pillars of the temple are the pillars of the Fornix. (Ref: 79)

The fornix is an Arc. It connects the left and right hemispheres of the brain. The holes in the bones of the skull that allow the energy that flows from it from to the left and to the right and back are called foramen in the medical dictionary. (For Amen). (Ref: 80)

I postulate that the energy centres (impedance changers) from the root to the crown transform the electricity / energy coming from the Earth into a high voltage. When it travels up through our root, sacral, solar, heart, throat, and pineal, if there is enough pure electricity, enough voltage, it hits the fornix (which means furnace) and lights up the whole body, mind, spirit in every dimension. Enlightenment. Lighting up.

Therefore, Ascension is the process of energy rising up through the body. It's so simple. There is no religion, no ism or schism about it. It just is. It is our natural state. Who we are. We are light and sound, energy that can neither be created nor destroyed, just transformed.

When we allow the natural forces within us to transform us, we go through the holy fire. A baptism of fire in the truest sense. This, therefore, puts the teachings of the second Adam, Atum, Amen into perspective.

There are only two commands that issue from the Amen.

1. Love your creator with your whole being;
2. Love everybody else the way the creator loves you.

Simple.

Sounds easy, but heck, it's anything but sometimes. However, the whole process is made easier if we follow the inner teachings. The INNER teachings. Everything lies within us. Everything we need to know, see, be, do, think — the whole thing. The Holy Spirit teaches us from within.

"But the Helper, the Holy Spirit, whom the Father will send in My name, He will teach you all things, and bring to your remembrance all things that I said to you." (Ref: 81)

Thus it could be said that the Bible scripts are a manual for life. They're an amazing guide on how to ascend and become free, and free indeed — which means in deed, all you do whilst on this Earth plane, beyond cause and effect, beyond duality or Karma. Living freely in an a-causal reality. The fact that the scripts have been misinterpreted and used as a spiritual hammer to beat people into submission is another story. However, those who truly question will find their own answers within. There is enough truth still left unedited to permeate even the hardest heart.

As far as I can see, the symbols of the Christ are all about becoming conscious and awakening to the incredible beings that we are.

I am taken back to 1994, when I visited the Vatican Museum. I was in Rome to visit a friend. I spent most of my days alone exploring the city, and most of my nights with Francesco, a rather handsome young man with a head full of deliciously dark curls and tanned skin. I walked around the Vatican staring at the naked sculptures (not lasciviously I hasten to add) and colourful pictures of holy men and women throughout the ages, each one with a golden halo painted around their heads. In a moment of revelation, I got it. I saw the deeper meaning of the halo: it symbolised pure enlightenment. I've always been able to see auras around people and thought everybody could—until I opened my mouth at the convent school and got shouted at. All of it became clear and literally blew my mind.

And so, to demystify the picture of Jesus and the sacred heart

(You can easily find a masterpiece picture of this online)

The blood is symbolised by the red robe. We know life is in the blood, the DNA of a person. The blood is transformed through the process of enlightenment. The DNA is activated: Jesus' blood speaks a better word. (Ref: Hebrews 12:24).

The crown of thorns symbolises the nerve surrounding the brain (also known as the crown of thorns) and is responsible for consciousness. The heart itself represents unconditional love that comes through the pain of awakening to self and all that is contained within. Why pain? Pain serves as a function to wake us up. The heart energy centre is the place where the cosmic energy

meets the earth energy. It is like a junction box, symbolised by the six-pointed star. It literally represents energy flowing up to the Godhead and down to the Earth. It is the key (think of this as a musical note) to the temple of Sol-om-on. It is the geometry of the heart. Nothing can work without this unconditional love. Love IS the key to life. It is a frequency, a flow, an electrical energy, and the igniter of the inner fire.

The open heart allows the energy of God to flow in all directions. Think of this symbol as such. The Cross and fire in the picture symbolise the inner fire, the furnace (fornix) esoterically known as Jesus, the Christ energy, and the cerebral spinal fluid crossing the vagus nerve as it rises up to the pineal gland, where, in the Bible, it states:

"The light of the body is the eye: if therefore thine eye be single, thy whole body shall be full of light." (Ref: Mathew 6:22)

How beautiful is that?

When the inner crucifixion takes place, all the core issues contained within the person come to the surface and that individual has to deal with them until natural ascension takes place. There is no agenda, no forcing, no religious doctrine, it is just who and what we are.

The symbols have been so totally misconstrued they have actually acted as red herrings, leading people astray and away from their true nature. The narrative is and has been anything but true. More, it could be said, devilish than Godly.

The fire has become hellfire, the cross has become a human sacrifice, and ascension has become a new age branded glossary. What a load of excrement!

So, it really is time to wake up the tree of life within us. The Arbor Vitae. The whole body of light within. To awaken every internal energy centre, our heart, torus field and activate the pineal and crown, lighting the Eternal flame (Fornix) to discover new worlds, Galaxies, and infinite multi-verses.

What? The Great Pyramid inside our head?

Pyramids inside our heads? (Please see Ref: 82) In esoteric circles, it is known that the Great pyramid represents the inside of our heads. The parallels that become obvious with this kind of overlay allow us to conclude that the King's Chamber is analogous to the Thalamus. The shaft points directly toward Orion or Osiris on one side, and Thuban on the other. The hidden chamber is found in the fornix.

(Image   from   The   Complete   Anatomy   App)

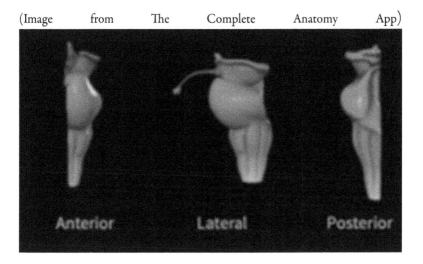

The Queen's chamber represents the hypothalamus. The Shaft points directly toward Sirius or Isis (left) and Ursa Minor (right).

It's extraordinary.

Let us take the skull. The outer dense irregular tissue that surrounds the brain is called the Dura Mater. (N.B.: Mater means Mother). It helps to protect the spinal cord, the cerebral spinal fluid (Christ oil), and other layers like the arachnoid and Pia mater. The arachnoid mater is like a web (arachnoid means spider) and acts as a veil between the Dura and Pia Mater. (In the Bible it talks about the veil in both the old and the New Testament and remember that Christ tore the veil — see Ref 83 . As previously mentioned, the cerebrum is symbolised as Cherubim (Angel wings as seen on the Arc of the Covenant) and the derivation of the word cere means covering. The job of a Cherubim is to cover and protect the mercy seat. In Exodus chapter twenty-five to the end of chapter twenty-six, we see a detailed explanation of the physiology of the brain, including the covering of the Ark of the Covenant, which is the pineal gland in the centre of the head and beneath it, the mercy seat. (Ref: 111 Image video)

Interestingly, there are protrusions on the medulla oblongata called pyramids. Who knew that such things existed and correlated so well with the external reality we all agree upon? When we examine the design of the Great Pyramid, we find a mind-blowing correlation to the brain. We notice that the King's chamber is in the Thalamus. The Aten or Amen's chamber. The place where the King is buried. The tomb. The Amen is Christ. The Queen's chamber is the Hypothalamus. We notice the hidden chamber, which is actually the Fornix, part of the Hippocampus. The Fornix, as we have previously defined, means furnace. It connects the left and right hemisphere of the brain enabling communication. The energy that travels between the two hemispheres is the foramen.

Theta brain waves resonate at about eight Hertz. Interestingly, below this brainwave, we find Delta Fornicis which resonates at about four Hertz. (Ref: 84) It could be said that this directly correlates with the constellation of the Fornax. Curiously, one of its stars is called Delta.

The Fornix is in the centre of the brain and just above the third ventricle. If you take the Fornax constellation as the centre of a star map or external brain, a fascinating thing happens. (Ref: 85)

Firstly, the shaft from the King's chamber angles directly toward the constellation of Orion (also known as Osiris — which means open eye). The angle of the shaft from the Queen's chamber leads directly to Sirius (also known as Isis or the Dog-star). On the other (right) side of the pyramid, there is a shaft from the King's chamber that points to Thuban, which used to be the Pole star about five-thousand years ago (3,000 B.C.) and a shaft from the Queen's chamber, the angle of which points to Ursa Minor.

Bearing in mind the four hertz delta wave frequency, I postulate that when we go into deep meditation, we reach beyond theta waves and resonate in a delta state, which is attuned to the frequency of the inner and outer constellations.

There are times when I close my eyes that all I see are infinite constellations of stars. I see them, feel them, hear them, and sometimes, fall upward into them. Their geometric angles create their resonance in relation to my own Fornix, and this, my human mind has interpreted as Angels singing, when in fact, it is angles resonating, which does not have quite the same romantic ring. The sacred geometry of life, the eternal flame, and constant God connection are all inside our own bodies. How amazing.

All my music has come from above, filtered through the cosmic layers and into the sounds of this dimension, carried through time and space into the hearts of those who would listen.

In the Biblical book of Job, chapter thirty-eight, verse seven, it talks about stars singing: "When the morning stars sang together, and all the sons of God shouted for joy." Which is what I feel when I wake up bursting with song, embodying the whole universe and singing it out so loudly the Earth shakes beneath my feet as I harmonise with all of nature. I close my eyes and within a few seconds I am out of my body and travelling through inner space to Andromeda, Orion, and indescribable places that are so far beyond words. Coming back into my body and fixing the broken washing machine, cleaning up after the animals, and peeling the spuds is occasionally more difficult than I would like it to be, but is made easier when the moment is shared with a loved one. No one knows how infinity plays its symphony in the mind of another. We all travel our allotted path through time and space in this dimension but can't know how the constellations sing their song through another's heart.

It seems to me that the melodies of wisdom and knowledge are transferred through space as radio waves into our heads and received by our inner antenna, our Ark (or arc) of the Covenant and our receiver and transmitter, the piezo-electric pineal gland.

Let us sing a love-song back to the source of all life, in harmonious worship of all creation.

Chapter Five

———

The Fornax Revelation: Master of the Timelines and Master of the Heavens

It was June of 2022 when I was invited to meet Vinny for an emotional release session in exchange for a radio interview. I reluctantly agreed; as a healer, I'm careful about whom I interact with. However, when we spoke on the phone, it was like talking to myself, and I felt like I had met a kindred spirit. Two months down the line and it turns out that we are like brother and sister.

I went into session with no preconceptions—except perhaps a vague concern as to what might or might not happen. Vinny helped me to release some big blocks that were still inside of me, holding me back. When this was done, I continued to deeply connect inwardly and then, it all started to unfold, and I was dancing in the light of the visible spectrum.

"I see you rainbow; I feel your energy, I see you."

After a few moments I was shooting up into the light.

I saw a strange sort of metal or silver shape in the sky. I telepathically communicated with it and realised it was a portal into another dimension. I switched it on, it activated, and created a vortex. I was staring into space.

I went in.

> "It's like our skies but the atmosphere is liquid. There's slight resistance as I move, but not much.
>
> I realise that I am in some kind of womb.

I see some sort of creature in front of me, but only glimpse its magnificence momentarily as she circles around me like an enormous piece of shimmering silk, embroidered with stars and galaxies. Everything is silent and there is a deep sense of tranquillity.

I allow myself to see what it is.

It looks like a sea creature. Deep silence. Then I said:

"This is a part of the universe where everything is liquid. It's not what we know as space, it's ... liquid. There are massive beings that are part of this space. I am in a huge womb. A massive, massive womb or something."

Vinny invites me to tune in even more.

I find myself standing in liquid space facing an enormous visage with huge eyes the size of Jupiter. The feeling is of incredible love: Divine love, all-embracing, permeating the core of my being. She embraces me with her eyes and I am just a speck. The space is vibrating and changing as I look at it.

"She comes into form as I look at her. She's the dragon Mother and she's embracing me. It feels amazing."

(Since this experience, I have researched the fornix and the Fornax Constellation. The picture at the beginning of this chapter made me gasp when I came across it on Wiki. It was the perfect representation of the Dragon Mother. I was moved to the core of my very being. There this beautiful creature was, a sort of Dragon-fish, and there was the symbol for the Fornax constellation.)

Vinny invited me to go deeper.

"We are going somewhere.... We're going through all sorts of thought formations. Where there's destruction and war they are holographic images, or sheets of film, projected onto some sort of two-dimensional screen. That's all they are, two-dimensional within this multi-dimensional space and they are replaying over and over, and we are going through all of these pages of a book or film screens. And they are like realities; there's millions of them. We choose. We choose what we go into. We choose; she doesn't choose for us, we do. It's almost like these holographic timelines are on repeat and they go around and around and around. And outside of all of those things there's this incredible space. It's not what we think it is. It is like a massive, massive wheel of infinite holographic realities. Each reality is a spoke in the wheel. We can pop into this one out of that one, but the holograms are set. That's what's set. As we go into whatever this hologram is, that is our life experience in relation to the hologram. It's the relationship to it that is the key to our growth on the journey we take. These holograms are re-runs because they're encapsulated within time and space. Outside of time and space there is something else which isn't that. So, I am getting that she is saying that some of these things have been set almost like a trap or malignancy. So you can get them to line up and you can become the Master of the timeline; you can go anywhere in that sphere. It's only a sphere. The idea is to become master of the timelines. Then that disappears — it goes. You become master of the timelines and all of it disappears for you."

Vinny: And then what happens?

"I was just seeing complete liberation. It's like we become more like her. We become a different shape, a different being. We no longer choose to go into that wheel. We become this amazing creature, which is like a multidimensional creature that can go anywhere in any dimension. It's not even dimensions, it's beyond dimensions.

"It feels like peace, but it also feels like there's more."

Vinny: If you really tune into "there's more," notice what happens.

Long silence.

"Fast-moving, pulsating energy, just energy. It has no colour or code. It's just energy. No personification.

"It's inverted. An inverted universe, like gravity in reverse. Like I'm somewhere, but it's outside. Like the inverse of reality. It feels weird. I'm on the outside looking in. There's a flow or energetic pull and I am not sure where that's going. I am looking into this inverted sphere. I'm on the other side of what I know as the multi-verse."

Vinny: Notice what happens now.

"I have been here before."

(What Vinny didn't know was that when I was seventeen I met Stephen Hawking at St. James's church in London. He took the whole assembly of people through a black hole into another universe. My universe was orange and inverted. I was unable to describe it in human terms. Now, thirty-five years later, I revisited it once more — as heard on the recording — and I still have few words to describe it.)

"There are rocks — a cluster here and a few there. Something that looks like a large cluster. It could be a place but it's not the same sort of shape as I'm used to. It's some sort of iron rock, red rock."

Long pause.

"It's like a desert: it's got red- and orange-coloured rocks everywhere. There's some sort of pulsating sound coming from underneath. I am going underneath. I am going through pools of magma; it's like a pulsating substance. I'm going through this kind of bubble, like a star-shield. I'm coming back to where I was on the edge. I can see a light cord, like a rope for me to pull myself back. I don't need to be there. I pull myself back through and into the liquid universe. It feels too far away; I don't need to be there. It's beyond my comprehension.

"It's the place where everything is. Is.

"Like an element. The elements, building blocks of universes.

"The building blocks of universes are the same; wherever you go it's the same. The elements are the same. It was an element. They have life, they have pulsations, vibrations, and universal energy, including the rock, the fire, it's what I am being shown. Everything has its journey — it's not the right word — but that's the closest I can get to it.

"And, we can draw on all of these things. (Literally).

"We can draw on all of these energies to create the (our) journey when we want to, choose to, to see things the way that we want to, to feel, to give birth to.

"So what I'm getting is that the timelines are a set of reactions and that certain vibrations always react the same way chemically. If we draw on the natural elements of the universe, we can master the timelines and go beyond them and build and create beyond the static images that are like photographs. We can build so much more than the holograms. And it's all there! It's all there. It's all there. And we are all part of one body. It is being written as we go. It's like we leave these holograms behind us once we've mastered (the timelines) and I'm getting that we leave an imprint on it.

(I asked if that means it can be changed.)

"We leave an imprint on it and then it can be changed when we master our elements.

"I'm back in an embrace with this creature. It feels familiar and peaceful. I am at peace.

"The world isn't what we think it is. It's nothing like what we think it is. The three-dimensional representation that we're able to perceive is nothing like what it actually is. We don't have the capacity to conceptualise what it is outside of personification because we don't understand what isn't. We can't comprehend what isn't, only what is and how that refraction happens through the mind as the light refracts into images. We see that. We can comprehend the light but we can't comprehend what isn't. The light is our life, we are that in our conceptual reality; but it isn't that... it is that, and it isn't that. What I'm seeing, I can't describe. So as we come into unification with all that is then the perception changes and we start to see what isn't.

"I get the sense or feeling of no fear."

Vinny: And that feeling of "just no fear" Do you accept that feeling to the core of your very being?

"Yes."

Vinny speaks to my superconscious mind.

"Because there is no fear, all the ideas I had are going, and because they are going, the reality I was living is dismantling. That's happening, and on another level, I get this deep sense of what my soul needs. That's okay, and as I expand, the needs are different, there are no needs; it's something else altogether. It's a sense of being. As I come into time, that's where the elements of ideas take place. The ideas that have been in my mind have been given to me and I haven't necessarily accepted them. I am being shown the nature of these ideas: they are built on fear. Because there's no fear, there's nothing to hold those ideas anymore. The resonance is changing now and my soul is crying out to be free of all of it: from that beautiful expanse, which is the isles, to the holographic images — all of that is clearing now, making way for truth, real infinite truth, which has no boundaries, restrictions, or constrictions. It is drawing upon the elements we have been given as gifts to pull into our reality. Everything we need is a natural refraction and reflection of the infinite, which is within each of us. I'm seeing that we pull it in like a magnetic flow — we pull it in. The language is a limitation and that's why it's so hard sometimes to pull it in. That is why no language is necessary: you can't speak that language. I'm being shown that our language is not the language of creation; it's the language of restriction.

"The language of creation is sound; that's where the music happens. There we are; that's it.

"Now, I'm in direct communication with the beings I met from Andromeda. They are saying that this is the point of creation: the utterance of sounds. I'm here to bring these sounds into manifestation. Knowing that things don't look the way I think they look, knowing that these ideas have gone because of no fear, knowing that there's no distance. There's no distance. It means that in space there's no distance or separation, there's only distance in our minds. There's only distance created by a lack of comprehension of energy and vibrations. There's only a separation in colour through the refraction of something. There's only distance when we use our natural eyes."

Vinny: So, distance and time are a projection of the mind?

"Yes, and that comes from what isn't, that place... I am coming back."

Vinny: With all the interdimensional wisdom, bringing everything back with you, connected to all those places, no distance, no time.

I came back to my body.

"When I think about creating a future aligned to my soul, it's a wide-open expanse. I choose. I choose not anybody else, so therefore I choose better, because it's not based on fear. It's like a book or books with lots of pictures — I just choose the ideas that resonate. No, I'm at the point where I am choosing ideas that work and serve; not ideas that are based on concepts. When the ideas were breaking, it was like all these walls dismantling, all the thought forms dissolving. It was a massive destruction. It was great!"

Result:

My inner experience was so profound to me that it's changed my perception of reality forever. I made such big shifts in the six weeks after that session that it's impossible to inhabit my old paradigm.

The revelation of the ties between the Fornix and Fornax is so mind blowing that I can hardly find the words to write what I see.

So, let's go back to the centre of the brain. We know that in the centre, the secret place, lies the pineal, which is made up of crystalline rods and cones and acts like an internal eye. We also know that Ammon's Horn (Hippocampus) is rather like a radio receiver. We know that the Fornix, at the top of Ammon's Horn, is the very centre of the head and is hollow like a cave. We also know that when ascension (enlightenment) occurs, the whole body is filled with light.

What is light? In Biblical Scripture is states that Light is God or God is light. What is light?

"This is the message we have heard from Him and announce to you, that God is Light, and in Him there is no darkness at all." (Ref: 86)

The science:

"Light is a kind of wave, somewhat like ocean waves or sound waves. Waves carry energy from one place to another. But light waves don't need water or air or anything to travel. They can move even in empty space (unlike sound waves). Light waves are made of a mixture of electricity and magnetism so they are called electromagnetic waves. These waves travel very quickly, about 186,000 miles (300,000 kilometers) per second. This means a beam of light could go 7 1/2 times around the world in one second." (Ref: 87)

Taking that Ammon (also Amen, Amun, Adam, Atum) or Atom, via the geometry of the Great Pyramid, is directly connected to Orion on one side and Thuban on the other, we can see that the inside of our brain directly correlates with the structure of the outer universe and galaxies. We are made in God's image.

"So, God created man in his own image, in the image of God he created him; male and female he created them." (Ref: 88)

The external universe and the internal universe are one, the very same design. Literally. Each part of the brain is found externally on every level of existence and has a function. What an exquisite creation.

Whoever designed the Great pyramid knew this.

As we are connected via our Ammon's horn (which, remember, translated means Jesus / Amun) to the external universe (our radio antennae) what exactly does it mean regarding Orion and Thuban?

Bill Donahue has done an enormous amount of research in this area and thank God I found him during my process of awakening.

The first thing to note is Orion. Or =Au = Gold

Ion = particle of light

Au = ion

Golden particle of light.

This constellation is also known as Osiris.

Os = Open

Iris = Eye

Open Eye.

Angles create a resonance. Resonance is a frequency and the frequency is sound. Sound is the carrier wave for intention, consciousness, etc.

The point I am making here is that everything external is mirrored internally — including every star and constellation. When we are internally activated, everything within us is filled with light, burning like the eternal flame.

The Fornix is the inner flame, the
Fornax is the outer. Set exactly between Orion (Osiris) and Sirius (Isis.)

On a personal note, I have a birth mark on my right index finger that is the symbol for Isis or Pineal and Ammon's Horn. It has taken until now to find out what on earth it meant. I hope you can see it in the picture. My hands have aged, but the symbol is still there. I knew people who knew what it was but refused to tell me, saying I wasn't ready to know. Perhaps they were right? Or perhaps they were there to steer me away from what I now know about myself. In ancient Roman mythology, the Fornax was the Divine personification of the oven and the Goddess of Bread (baked in the oven).

In the picture at the beginning of the chapter, we see the anthropomorphic representation of the Fornax. The beautiful creature in my mind whom I called the Dragon mother. Half fish, half dragon, swimming in the liquid universe.

I have no science to back it up, but I experienced the universe as made of liquid; certainly something that reminded me of water. There are some theories that this is true but nothing easily found to verify what I saw and felt during my session.

(Do your own research. Here's a link: Ref: 89)

In the book of Genesis in the Bible, it talks about the waters being separated from the waters. In that way it would make sense. In fact, our brains are full of liquid, so perhaps it's another case of as above so below. The knowledge is within, so I am not saying you will have the same experience as I did.

Psalterium

Medical dictionary: com•mis•sur•a for•'ni•cis [TA] the triangular subcallosal plate of commissural fibres resulting from the converging of the right and left fornix bundles that exchange numerous fibres and that curve back in the contralateral fornix to end in the hippocampus of the opposite side. (Ref: 90)

The Psalter is a beautiful stringed instrument, rather like a harp or lyre.

In the picture of the Fornax constellation, we see the symbol of the harp, which of course is the Fornix / Fornax.

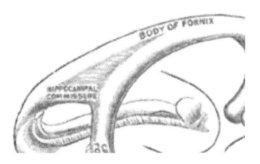

IN THE BIBLE, DAVID soothed King Saul's soul when he played the harp. This, I believe means that we are soothed by tuning in to the universe via our Pineal/Hippocampus.

As everything is manifested from the invisible realms into three dimensions through us, the external manifestation takes on the shape of an instrument — the harp.

I have never heard an ugly sounding harp. Isn't it interesting that harps and angels are so often seen together. The wings (Cerebrum), the Harp, Psaltarium, The Angel, geometric angles — taken together in this context, it begins to seem that the symbols are each different takes on the same concept.

In my twenties, I had the most beautiful experience of hearing Angels singing. The sound was extraordinary. I tried so hard to write a song that reflected the sound but nothing came close. In my personal experience, the inspiration to make music comes from these angels and resonances. These are frequencies emanating from the stars in the form of light and scalar energy.

From the Angelic tones of stars singing, I am led on to something less appealing: Zion or Z'ion.

The letter Z is symbolic for weaponisation. This is evidenced on Russian tanks and is also a symbol for the swastika and black sun.

Let us comprehend that all is frequency. All is light and sound and that includes positive and negative vibrations. When we examine the following symbols, let us think of them as sonic frequencies rather than incomprehensible patterns that have no meaning save to the initiated few or those who would assign limited beliefs to them for example: The Swastika or Cross.

By passing a sonic current through water, one can observe Faraday waves. This can be seen visibly and according to their frequency and tone, manifest patterns accordingly. (Ref: 91) Han Jenny's Cymatics, Masaru Emoto's water experiments, and other sound experiments all show the same things. The shape of sound is made visible, and it is universal.

"When fluid enclosed by a container is subjected to a vertical oscillation, standing waves arise. These standing waves, which depend on reflections from the edge of the container, are known as Faraday waves." (Miles and Henderson, 1990)

Please watch the unlisted video illustrating the universal sonic frequencies and their symbolic representations. (Ref: 92) You will see a whole new world open up in front of your eyes. When I first saw this, I realised that what I had been staring at for over fifty years, trying to fathom their meaning became clear and opened a new reality. This insight made me realise that every word, thought, dream, good deed, bad decision, negative utterance, and so on resonated throughout the whole multiverse and that the words of the scripts, no matter which brand, were all saying the same thing: Everything is frequency and the strongest frequency of all is love. That's what it all leads to.... Love......

So why is there so much trouble on the Earth Plane?

Chapter 6

―――

The 'Z' in the Tree

After the revelations of the previous chapter, I came to innerstand that we are electric beings and receive and give energy to and from the Earth, to and from each other and to and from the sky. That being the case, I asked myself "for what purpose?" and "Why?"

In our natural state, we give and receive freely. This realm of existence is set up for us to flow freely in union with creation. So why then, is there so much trouble? What's the cause of all this?

As far as I can see, history is literally "his story" and changed at the drop of a hat to suit the current climate regardless of evidence contrary to the desired narrative. This either drags us all into a poor representation of life or the truth of the present moment, which is our own recreation. Yesterday and tomorrow are created through all we are doing or being today. And if, as a whole species, what we are doing/being today is set within and restricted by a fake narrative, a fake history, and controlled thinking, a fake education, fake rules and regulations issued by fake authorities, then what is real? If yesterday has gone and our short-term memory is based on a subjective reality, then what is actually really happening, if anything? And who's responsible?

During my sessions with Vinny, I realised that some find it hard to comprehend what is not, the darkness, anti-matter, the apparent nothingness, but it's there that we might find the innerstanding of what is. It is right there where the treasure of darkness lies.

As creatures who respond to light, we have been programmed to be afraid of the dark. Yet that's where we need to shine our lights the most. There's nothing to fear, we carry the light. We close our eyes and what do we see but darkness; yet there's a whole multiverse of experiences to be had when we open our inner eyes and see through the darkness and what is not into what is.

In order for us to turn the lightbulb on, we have to know we have one, we have a switch to it, and we know where the heck it is. Then we have to clean ourselves up from the stuff we have been consciously (or unconsciously) consuming physically, mentally, emotionally, and spiritually. Navigating a clean path through the mire can be a challenge sometimes.

So what is the light bulb and where is the switch?

From previous chapters, we know that each energy centre is an impedance changer and resonates in alignment with the spectrum of light that shines through us via the prism of the organic mind. Our crystal prism is our pineal gland and fornix. The light of God or the universe comes in directly as photons and shines through our whole body according to our capacity. The more we clean up, the more capacity we have, making room for more photons to flow out into this realm, or wherever we may be.

So imagine this: The photons we receive are beamed from all over the universe. For example: Orion's belt contains a star called Alnitak, which has a visual magnitude of 2.0 and an absolute magnitude of -6.0. It has thirty-three times the Sun's mass and a radius twenty times that of the Sun. It is the brightest class 0 star in the sky. Imagine the light from this one star alone beaming into our pineals and filling us with divine intelligence. (For more star facts see reference 93.)

If everything outside us is replicated and connected to the inside, then the light frequencies of each sun, moon, and star resonates within us in an energetic symphony, either harmoniously or in dissonance, through every Atom, every organ, and all apparency of matter.

Imagine for a moment that every star has a cosmic function. It'd be very surprising if they didn't, as all creation seems to exist for a reason. Imagine my surprise when I found my own star family in the constellation of Andromeda. Prior to my session with Vinny, I didn't even know whether Andromeda was a planet, star, place, or ship. Imagine how I felt when I learned that the Andromedans had been sending me musical and spiritual directions all my life. Apparently, the true name for this star field is something else unknown to most of us here on Earth.

Imagine now, the geometric angles between us and the stars. These angles are what we know as angels and it could be said, are messages of light direct from the heavens. This coincides with all I have written in chapter two to do with our fourth- and fifth-dimensional astrology.

When we look up into the night sky, what are we really looking at? I shall come back to this point. For now, let us examine the meaning of the letter Z and how this might be having an impact upon us.

The letter Z is very interesting. It is currently the symbol for weaponisation and can be found on Russian military tanks. It's also the symbol for the swastika.

"It became a militarist[1] symbol used in Russian propaganda and by Russian civilians as a sign of support for invasion. Outside Russia, the symbol has been banned from public display in various countries. The "Z" symbol has been pejoratively called a zwastika or zwaztika, in reference to the Nazi swastika,[15[2]] or pejoratively in Russian and Ukrainian as "zig" or "zigi" (Russian: зиг, зигии) in reference to *Sieg Heil*[3]." (Ref: 94)

Let's look a little more closely at the swastika and its different meanings.

It could be said that in the same way that the body has been demonised, so has the symbol of the swastika. It makes one wonder why everything beautiful has been turned into something ugly.

The definition of the word swasti in Sanskrit means: "source of all auspiciousness" and also refers to welfare, fortune, and prsperity.

---

1. https://en.wikipedia.org/wiki/Militarist

2. https://en.wikipedia.org/wiki/Z_(military_symbol)%2523cite_note-zwastika-15

3. *https://en.wikipedia.org/wiki/Sieg_Heil*

In fact, in all Asian cultures, the swastika represents sun, light, good fortune, infinite bliss, and the source of all creation.

In Ancient Egyptian, ka (kɑ) n. was the spiritual part of an individual believed by ancient Egyptians to survive the body after death. (NB: Mer-ka-ba).

Regardless of language, the original meaning of the swastika was positive.

The Thule society, we are told, used the symbol to represent the black sun whilst the Phoenicians used it to represent the White Sun and Holiness.

It begs the question: Is the subjective interpretation meaningful?

If the Russians see Z as complete victory through violence, the Neo-Nazis the same but for different reasons, yet the Hindus place it above their doorways to bring good fortune, confusion ensues. We know from reference 92 that the swastika is a resonant frequency or sound.

Let us dig a little deeper in a different direction and have a bit of fun with it. Please go to the reference marked 92.1 Fun

Knowing that the energy centres of the body are impedance changers and therefore can be measured in Ohms (or Oms) and knowing that Z is also the symbol for electrical shock vector, when all the occult mystery is removed, we have something else altogether. (We have David Bowie... ha ha ha)

It brings a whole new meaning to Ziggy Stardust. (I thought some comic relief at this point wouldn't go amiss). Don't forget your makeup boys!

We can see what he was doing here very clearly representing the single eye. He was telling us. So now we comprehend once again that the truth is hiding in front of us and that it is far simpler than people would have us believe. The letter Z is also known as Ziggi and symbolises the Electrical Vector.

Resistor symbol

What is a resistor?

"A resistor is an electronic component that limits the current in an electronic circuit. The resistor also can set as voltage divider but output voltage swing when connecting to low resistance load." (Ref: 95)

As previous postulated, our energy centres are the impedance changers, and we are set rather like a circuit board with resistors and capacitors. Each chakra has its function and purpose on a multi-dimensional level.

"Resistance vs. Impedance — The main difference between Resistance and Impedance is their Alternating Current (A.C.) and Direct Current (D.C.) currents. While resistance controls the flow of AC and DC current, Impedance just determines the alternative current flow. It means that impedance is only used in AC systems and does not have any use in DC diagrams. Another considerable difference for identifying resistance vs. impedance is that impedance can be combined with inductive reactance[4], resistance, or capacitance reactance. While resistance only means the resistance of an instrument. We must know their application in AC and DC circuits before understanding the resistance vs. impedance term. It should be considered that both calculation method of value is the same with R=V/I equation (Ohm's Law[5])." (Ref: 96)

I postulate that our inner resistors manifest as blocks we find in our basic, inherited programming. It is our job, upon awakening, to repurpose these blocks and through the process of neuroplasticity or neurogenesis, reprogram the old circuitry. Awakening to ourselves enables the God-particle (or Christ) within our DNA to be activated. To qualify this, in 1998, Pjotr Garjajev, a Russian scientist, discovered that DNA could be changed through the power of language and sound. (Ref: 100) To take the research further, as a voice specialist, I found that we respond best to the sound of our own voices. It's for this reason I started my business of Calibrated Affirmations, to help people activate their own healing through the power of the sound of their own voice. (Ref: 101)

What is an Electric field?

An electric charge is a property of matter that causes two objects to attract or repel depending on their charges (positive or negative).

---

4. https://en.wikipedia.org/wiki/Electrical_reactance

5. https://en.wikipedia.org/wiki/Ohm's_law

An electric field is a region of space around an electrically charged particle or object in which an electric charge would feel force.

An electric field is a vector quantity and can be visualized as arrows going toward or away from charges. The lines are defined as pointing radially outward, away from a positive charge, or radially inward, toward a negative charge.

So it could be said that the Z in the tree symbolises the electric charge of the ions, particles, and atoms in our bodies.

So what if we join these symbols together to make Zion? No demonisation. No occult nonsense to throw us off. Just simple deduction.

What if the true meaning of Zion is to be fully charged, not weaponised? Taking away the distortion, it could be said that when we are fully charged, we are empowered, enlightened, ascended. The light is on.

What is Zion? Etymology:

Middle English Sion, from Old English, citadel in Palestine, which was the nucleus of Jerusalem, from Late Latin, from Greek Seiōn, from Hebrew Ṣ īyōn

Zion in the Bible refers to the City of God. The city of God is within us. Jerusalem is us. "Then Solomon assembled the elders of Israel and all the heads of the tribes, the leaders of the fathers' houses of the people of Israel, before King Solomon in Jerusalem, to bring up the ark of the covenant of the Lord out of the city of David, which is Zion." (Ref: 97)

Sol (Sun) Om (Ohm) On (City of light). Twelve Tribes — twelve cranial nerve (pairs = twenty-four elders). Ark of the Covenant — the Pineal and Hippocampus (Arc) City of David = Zion.

Roughly taken together, all of this translates as the internal process of enlightenment (Solomon) where the electrical current flows through the energy centres/cranial nerves/neurological systems (Zion) into the pineal (Ark / Fornix).

This is all about building the temple, which of course is inside our own body/skull. If you read on, you will find in the next chapter in the Bible, (1 Kings 9) that David has reached the Godhead.

The Lord said to him: "I have heard the prayer and plea you have made before me; I have consecrated this temple, which you have built, by putting my Name there forever. My eyes and my heart will always be there." (Ref: 98)

So how does this all fit together?

Zion is the city of God. Our inner temple, our body. Positively charged ions. God particles. Z-ion.

The Z in the tree (of life) is the electrical vector. The flow of energy up and down our bodies. Our electro-magnetic spheres. Our Biofields or Auras. We are like multidimensional balls of energy, electricity, photons, ions, light. Beings of light and sound. We are a miraculous creation.

Recently, I have been fortunate enough to have my cell voltage jump started through the use of Professor Andrew Hague's Cellsonic machine. I suffered a knee injury some time ago, followed by stress, bereavements, broken relationships, pain, loss, and challenges so mountainous, even the toughest of friends have wondered how I didn't break. I didn't, but my body wasn't happy.

When our voltage gets reduced through stress, bad nutrition, toxic emotions, scars, unhealthy teeth and bones, bad relationships, and so on, it can lead to chronic disease (dissonance) in the body, mind, and emotions. Some manifest cancer, others chronic pain, and others, like me, put all of the painful problems into a big fibroid the size of a large cabbage. Over the years, I have had various parts of my body removed, which has all been part of this deep awakening and connection to God. The deep yearning for love and to innerstand why I am here has caused me to go beyond all my doubts and limitations into a place of complete faith and gratitude.

When I was thirty five I had a basal cell carcinoma removed from my leg. I listened to Ella Fitzgerald on my headphones as the surgeon removed the offending protuberance and neatly sewed the skin together like a nice pair of curtains. I watched as she did it feeling nothing but the rhythm of the swing beat in my ears. Had I known what was to follow this, I might not have been so blasé about my future self and my dear body who, through it all, has endured more than its fair share of burdens.

A few years after, I had a difficult childbirth, ending in a c-section followed by two years of sickness and a decade of legal shenanigans. As well as growing the most beautiful child, I grew the large fibroid the size of a six-month-old foetus, which had to be removed along with my womb. The operation went wrong, as the surgeon did not sew me up properly like the previous one had, so I had to go back in. But it didn't stop there. I had Bell's palsy, which appeared two days before Halloween (very timely) and a special musical performance, which I found hilarious. Fortunately a very skilful cranial-sacral osteopath helped me to remove the symptoms in two weeks when it usually takes a lot longer for most people. There is more and frankly, one would have thought I might have taken some notice by now, but no, I soldiered on. On to a few years later, a lot more stress and another hospital visit with acute pancreatitis. A gall-stone had got stuck and was causing me a lot of pain. I was on my way out. Nine days nil by mouth and a four-year-old I did not want to be separated from. I was literally brought to my knees. Here is what I wrote from my hospital bed whilst on a diet of morphine and prayer.

"As I sit across from the hospital bed on the opposite wall, I am staring back in time to when I was last here on the same ward at the same time of year, with the same nurses having had my fibroid and womb removed.

"As I allow my eyes to survey the latest patient in the bed (there have been three since I arrived) it's like looking back into the land of Egypt from the promised land. The chasm could not be wider. I am staring back to a time that symbolised a lifetime of abuse, pain, and sorrow. What has followed can only be described as a Divinely ordained clean-up job complete with spiritual 'Domestos' and surgical procedures that have had to be employed as a last resort. It's been a week since my gallbladder decided to send a stone into my pancreas causing inflammation in the form of pancreatitis. And what a journey across the Red Sea. As I lie here, my life is swirling before me in a Helix-shaped hologram. I watch, as scene after scene is played out. I listen, as the resonance seems to vibrate through my soul. I know I have a lifetime to condense into non-linear time. Thoughts are like the 1970s Space Monkeys that look tiny until you immerse them in water and suddenly, they magically expand into big, colourful paper fish. I've come from a fruitless existence into the hope of a life filled with love, wisdom, and understanding. The false 'me's' are all shattered and broken into pieces and the real me is emerging. The person that God made me to be.

"Someone told me to draw a line in the sand and I thought I had done a few years ago. The trouble with sand is that it's not permanent. The tide tends to come in and wash the line away repeatedly. The wind blows and causes a storm, and the sand gets into everything and permeates all areas of life from finance to health and even one's bed. Sand is not an acceptable currency. It seems like no matter how many lines I draw, it makes no difference as I am not in control of this experience. My equivalent is turning my eyes toward heaven, where my help comes from. It's only Divine help that can release me from this prison of fear, condemnation, pain, sorrow, and the bondages of Earthly life. As I watch, surprising events unfold before me. I am in awe of how God is working through my life as He tunes me up as His musical instrument that I might speak and sing His will into being. It's a painful rest.

"It takes time to rest. The musical definition of rest is a place where nothing happens for a signified number of beats and bars. The definition for rest in my personal life is: The ever-elusive thing that never happens because there is always something I should be doing as a single parent. I've been through a lot, more than some, less than others. A lot for me, and, it seems, to the onlookers. A lot for anyone inhabiting a human body. Life is never boring, in fact, I would not recognise boredom as I have never had the luxury of it."

"Today is my seventh day in hospital with acute pancreatitis. They could not operate as I have been too inflamed, so I have had to lie in bed for a whole week. The fact that I have been pricked, prodded, poked, scanned, radiated, drugged, and wired to machines is neither here nor there. My veins are so small I have been used as a pin cushion as most of the nurses have not been able to find anything wide enough in which to place a cannula. The portable scanner has had to be brought in on numerous occasions as I watch in anticipation of another day of experts playing 'find a vein'. They say a change is as good as a rest; although it's not quite the holiday I was hoping for, but when you're as stubborn and tenacious as I am at carrying on regardless, God takes more drastic measures. I have been forced to fast for six days and I am no longer hungry. My gallstone has passed.

"Interestingly my father used to tell me "You've got a lot of gall" and I thought it was a compliment meaning I was brave and strong. Today, after a lifetime of not knowing the concept and meaning of the word gall, I looked it up and found the truth. Something bitter to endure, bitterness of spirit, rancour, brazen boldness coupled with impudent assurance and insolence. He meant I was the last part of the previous sentence, which was about right in his regard.

"I have been praying for nine months to forgive my oppressors and know something has happened in spirit. This has translated into the physical and the last bit of all my ugly bitterness is being surgically removed. All of the definitions of gall have applied to me owing to the kind of life I have experienced. I never saw it as a bad thing but when I get down to it, I have to admit that I have hated some of the things that have happened to me. I have carried them around, well hidden behind my hope for a better future and a fear of repetition. You can hide a lot behind synthesised hope. Yes, a hope of what you think you should have and the reality of what you've got to deal with.

"My over-eating started during pregnancy as the relationship with the father of my child turned sour. It's been nearly ten years of my life, dealing with the rotten fruits born in the spirit of this man and directed toward me, and forty-eight years of abuse from my own father. I am not without fault, but I endured a loveless childhood and life until I gave birth to my child.

"I've just spoken to the nurse followed by the surgeon. They have found something on my liver that shouldn't be there. Is this the end for me? This was found in the C.T. scan and is an unexpected blow. The operation will happen tomorrow at the same time as the father of my child will be in court for sexual abuse and a final decision regarding future access. I can see the court room from the hospital window and feel a strange symmetry as I gave birth one floor above from where I am laying.

"Sometimes it all gets too much when your joy, hope, freedom, love, and health is taken, and you begin to see how much there actually is to be grateful for. There are times when I feel squashed, punished, attacked, cursed, and have a whole lot to break through. Only God can do this, so I am asking... but I am blessed, and people have been to see me, brought flowers and I have a large bunch of delicious grapes on my table to look forward to, which will be nice after seven days of hospital jelly. My biggest blessing is my daughter. I dreamed about her before I even conceived her and saw the first twenty-four years of her life as if on a screen. Nothing can describe the love that I have for her, how I want her to have a happy life and not have to go through what I have gone through. I am feeling worried that this is it. I ask the nurses but they are not allowed to answer."

"Friends sympathise but no one knows the depth of the pain I have experienced and at last I am not holding it in, my tears are flowing now, washing it all away...."

Since that moment in hospital, I have moved on so far that I hardly recognise my own words. Truly comprehending that I am an electric being, full of the light of Christ, connected to the infinite has helped me on this healing journey. In fact, seeing all of this has been because of the gift of the pain and trauma I experienced. I can honestly say that I would never have had to dig so deep had I not experienced that kind of suffering. I am deeply grateful and as I become more conscious and closer to God, I take more and more responsibility for each thought, word, and deed, in every moment. This was my crown of thorns moment.

The myrrh in my own soul was transformed into honey by walking through the purging fires of a deeper spiritual baptism The deep pain I experienced turned me inside out and created a mighty warrior, my truest weapon being love and compassion, not just for my child or my abusers but also for myself. I have, over the last decade, learned to love, forgive and appreciate all that I am and have been on this plane of existence. I have let go of deep inner blocks, such as materialism, intellectualism, perfectionism, status, money and loneliness and of course there are many other things to work on.

My solitude has turned into a peaceful union with God; the pain is now compassion for all living creatures, the myrrh is, like the story in the Old Testament in Judges 14:14 that says: 'out of the strong came forth sweetness'.

Crown of Thorns:

Whenever I ask a question of God, I always get amazing answers. They come in all sorts of ways from signs, words, songs, visions, intuitions, and sometimes, by catching a random program on the radio. In 2018, I heard a radio program about the latest discoveries in neurology. Scientists have discovered a nerve in mice that circumnavigated the whole skull. They said it was responsible for consciousness. I decided to look it up and was shocked by its image. I said to myself: My God, it looks like the crown of thorns!" And that is exactly what it is. It is called the crown of thorns and is found in us humans too.

And then, I saw it all. All the mockery I had experienced outside the court as my father told the whole waiting room every single misdemeanour and sin, he thought I had committed for two and a half hours while we waited to go in to be judged. Scoffing and laughing at me with his cohorts before he testified against me and lost, owing to his part in the perjury and abuse that both he and the father of my child had committed. That every single accusation he placed upon his own daughter's head was something he (and the father of my child) was found guilty for. All the lies, deception, and sorrow he inflicted on me never stuck; both fathers were shamed as their Masonic initiations got them nowhere when standing in the face of Christ. The images in my mind of Christ bleeding under the crown of thorns impressed upon my spirit as they belittled, insulted, and ridiculed me in front of my pastor and friends who came to support me. My pastor saying, "Don't let them see you are affected" and then afterwards saying, "I have never heard or seen anything like that in my whole life. It might take a while to get over it." The crown of thorns pressing into me as I became more and more awakened to myself, life, spirit, and a new world I had never inhabited before. I knew that this was a deep spiritual initiation and revelation. I knew in that moment that the symbol of this incredible nerve was responsible for awakening, becoming conscious, and that the pain I had experienced was an incredible gift that served to wake me up completely. I knew then and know now that pain, when realised, is the gift of purging and redemption. When Christ is consciously permitted to infuse every part of the self, the whole being, transformation and ascension is the result.

The outplaying of the story of Christ was literally transforming my consciousness, my mind, soul, heart, and body and the words from the script, so deeply infused from the age of seven, were, through a spiritual osmosis, cleansing every atomic particle.

From the spiritual battle in court, to the hospital bed, I knew that every part of me was being transformed and that my genetic line was being purged, right the way back to Adam, the first atom. All my ancestors were being liberated as my internal crucifixion took place and the beginning of the comprehension of who and what we are began to blossom.

As I sit here half a decade later, not so very far away from both the courthouse and the hospital, the birds are singing in the sunrise and another Spring is only a month or so away. The trees I planted last year look as if they might do well and there is peace in my heart. We made it through.

I shall always be grateful to those who stood by me through this process. So many miracles happened and continue to do so as I take a closer walk with truth, faith, love, and Spiritual wonder. I shall never forget the two African women who taught me how to truly pray. To pray like an African means that you have to start praying every Monday night from 10pm til 4am, for three and a half years. Pray so fiercely that your wig flies across the room, leaving your stocking afro underneath. Dearest Rachel and Matilda literally kicked every demonic entity out of me and showed me what true love for God is all about. Ladies, you will never know how much you mean to me and I thank you from the bottom of my heart. Thank you.

> There were times when all I had to pay the rent was the £2.00 in my purse. Once, knowing I had nothing, I used the last £2.00 for an ice cream and took my daughter to the beach thinking that if I was going down, then at least we would have some nice memories of playing

in the sand and park. On the way back from a day at the beach I saw a sign in a window as I was stuck in traffic, and it said: "Expect a miracle." "Look Mummy! Look at the sign!" We both smiled and something in me knew that God was speaking to us. When we got home, I unlocked the door. It wouldn't open properly, as there was something in the way. I picked it up. It was an envelope with "Love from God" written on it. I opened it and there was £500.00 in cash. The exact amount that I was short on the rent. I cried, just like I am now as I remember all the incredible moments that have led me here.

Chapter 7
The Inner Constellations

———

Many years ago, I realised that everything in the universe and in spirit is reflected internally and then externally as a latent effect on the Earth plane. All things are happening simultaneously. When they harmonically align, we gain mastery over the physical world and our universe, or innerverse.

I had no idea that my realisation was more than a subjective meandering and that every detail of creation is perfectly mirrored, from the stars in the sky to each animal, bird, insect, plant, element, and organ of our body.

This enormous symphony of sound hums itself into form, turning particles and waves into myriad harmonic galaxies, life forms, and raw elements. We, as part of the whole, sing our own unique DNA to the rhythm of our heartbeat, the song of our soul, like diamonds refracting the light of our sun, upheld by our sacred geometric location in space at the time of our birth, the angles of light creating the resonance of our being, manifest into physical form.

In previous chapters I have mentioned the Fornix and the Fornax. The inner fire and the outer furnace or Eternal Flame. The place where, when there is enough energy or voltage, everything lights up and awakening / neurogenesis / restoration / healing ensues. This is what I mean when I say: "It's time to wake up the trees." Wake up the tree of life inside our whole body, from the Arbor Vitae to each energy centre. We are the trees of life.

In some Pentecostal Christian circles, it is taught that the tree of life is Jesus (Ref: Genesis 2:9) which is true biologically as explained previously. The Arbor Vitae is attached to the Medulla Oblongata and the Pons. Upon examining the Pons, we find some very interesting images. Please see the video in the next Endnote. (Ref: 99)

So, the question is: what are we looking at when we look into the night sky? Could it be the mind of the Creator, in which we are made in the image? I wonder. Could every star and galaxy really be within us? Literally?

Let's examine the definition of the word Galaxy: "any of the systems of stars and interstellar matter that make up the universe. Many such assemblages are so enormous that they contain hundreds of billions of stars." (Ref: Britannica)

The derivation of the word Galaxy comes from the Greek word *galakt*, which means milk, hence the Milky Way. Once again, I am taken to the mammillary bodies of the brain, which are linked to the hippocampus and fornix. Mammillary means breast. (Ref: 105)

In my sessions with Vinny, I discovered that my innerverse was made of liquid (milky way) and that the Fornax / Fornix was symbolised universally by a dragonfish, just like the one I met during my session. I saw that we are electric beings. In order to reach so-called enlightenment, we need enough voltage to start the flow or current both in our physical and

etheric bodies. Without enough voltage, dissonance or disease might ensue.

I followed up that learning with a meeting with Professor Andrew Hague. He invented the Cellsonic machine, which is known to cure cancer and many other diseases through passing volts (25,000) through the cells of the body. The right voltage is so important for our physical health but, without the right mindset, according to Andrew, healing does not necessarily last. If your mind is reset through meditation, exercise, fun, laughter, joy, and play, healing is complete and stays that way. The Professor explained that it has to be both physical and mental. This is in accordance with all I have been saying when it comes to the anatomy of faith, belief, trust, love, joy, etc., etc. They are all frequencies and create a resonance (or, if lacking, a dissonance) within the electromagnetic field of the body.

In Andrew Hague's paper: "The Electric Properties of Cancer Cells," he explains:

"The cells of the body are composed of matter. Matter itself is composed of atoms, which are mixtures of negatively charged electrons, positively charged protons and electrically neutral neutrons. When an electron is forced out of its orbit around the nucleus of an atom the electron's action is known as electricity. An electron, an atom, or a material with an excess of electrons has a negative charge. An atom or a substance with a deficiency of electrons has a positive charge. Like charges repel unlike charges attract. Electrical potentials are created in biological structures when charges are separated. A material with an electrical potential possesses the capacity to do work."

The Professor goes on to explain that coils have a greater inductance than straight conductors. Think about this in terms of cells and body structures.

"...a number of membrane proteins as well as DNA consist of helical coils, which may allow them to electronically function as inductor coils. Also, some research that I have seen also indicates that biological tissues may possess superconducting properties. If certain membrane proteins and the DNA actually function as electrical inductors, they may enable the cell to transiently produce very high electrical voltages." (Hague. A)

As I read through 'the science', I realised that what I have seen intuitively is actualised in reality, confirming that it is all written within us. No matter what is happening externally or how much interference occurs, ultimately, nothing can destroy the truth of who and what we are. We just need to be activated.

The Professor reveals:

"Activation of cell membrane receptors that act as antennas for certain windows of frequency and amplitude leading to the concepts of electromagnetic reception, transduction and attunement."

This is directly in alignment with musical attunement, sonic healing, and energy balancing. We all know how awful it is to listen to an orchestra playing out of tune, a perfect metaphor for tuning up our bodies, the innerverse and the multi-verse. It also means that every cell of our body is an aerial or receiver and that the excess information and energy is stored in the magnetic field. This adds weight to what we are carrying, or should I say, uniquely carrying, as each one of us is like no other, which is extraordinary, in itself.

Our voltage is activated and enhanced through cleansing our electromagnetic fields and energy centres. Through this daily practice we maintain a healthy organism and regenerate. This can also be done very simply through the use of a tuning fork or by singing or listening to specific sonic frequencies. On the other end of the complexity spectrum are amazing pieces of equipment such as the CellSonic machine, which have also shown remarkable regeneration effects. (Ref: 106)

Why, you might ask.

Each of our seven energy centres (seven churches) has their own voltage and note or frequency. I don't like to be prescriptive here because we are unique, and all tuned slightly differently. However, it has been demonstrated that particular frequencies create a more complete visible form than others (for example 432 Hz when compared to 440Hz.) This is a science fact, not foo-foo.

Bearing in mind that we are seventy-five percent water, think about what happens when we are constantly listening to music that is attuned to 440Hz rather than 432Hz. It's "mis"-creating within our waters. We know that the prolonged effect of dissonance creates DISease. (Ref: 107)

On the subject of tuning, remember that the symbol of the Lyra (or harp) represents the hippocampus and the fornix? The story of David and King Saul in the Bible illustrates the use of music to soothe anxiety and fear. (Ref: 109)

15 And Saul's servants said unto him, Behold now, an evil spirit from God troubleth thee.16 Let our lord now command thy servants, which are before thee, to seek out a man, who is a cunning player on an harp: and it shall come to pass, when the evil spirit from God is upon thee, that he shall play with his hand, and thou shalt be well.22 And Saul sent to Jesse, saying, Let David, I pray thee, stand before me; for he hath found favour in my sight.23 And it came to pass, when the evil spirit from God was upon Saul, that David took an harp, and played with his hand: so Saul was

refreshed, and was well, and the evil spirit departed from him. (Ref: 110)

The evil spirit from God was upon him? How interesting.

Firstly, let's define the name David, which means beloved or dearly loved. Secondly, Saul means to ask for.

Translated: The evil spirit (bad energy) from God (infinite energy, neither good nor bad) had been noticed by the nervous system (servants) had been summoned (Saul) and was troubling/creating a dissonance. Command the servants (which would be the twelve cranial nerves) to find a clever way of participating in activating (playing the lyra, which is in the centre of the fornix) the hippocampus (memory storage centre) in order to heal. The beloved (David) heals the dissonance. To state it more clearly: the frequency of love heals the problem.

It is all about frequencies, energies, voltage, and attention or at-tension. Whatever we focus upon comes into being and creates an effect. Sometimes, owing to low voltage, we are predisposed to lower forces, which create trouble in our mind, body, and spirit. Sometimes, our cells (every cell is a receiver) pick up some dissonance and our bodies suffer as a result, causing pain and anxiety. The above scripture is clearly telling us how to soothe our troubles. It could be said that it happens both internally and externally, playing out in our realities as the stories we are telling ourselves. The programmes we are running that have been inherited or are fixed as holographic experiences, potentialities, or possibilities. Sometimes, we re-run them over and over until we learn to heal ourselves and make a better choice.

How many times in the past have we had relationships with different people and yet, they all possess the same qualities in a different skin? Or the same old thing happens over and over until we change our storyline. Sometimes, our memories (stored in the hippocampus/fornix) replay over and over until we are in a chronic negative state and our voltage is running low. PTSD would be an example of this. However, knowing all we now know about how sound and light affects everything, there is no excuse for us to remain in the doldrums. It is time to awaken to our true nature which, I believe is good (God).

As I examine the symbol of the harp or Lyra, I am taken to the constellation of Lyra and in anatomy, the middle portion of the ventral surface of the fornix of the brain.

Lyra represents the lyre of Orpheus, the musician and poet in Greek mythology who met his end at the hands of the Bacchantes. When he passed, his lyre was thrown into a river. Zeus sent an eagle to get the lyre and placed both of them in the sky.

When we examine the story of the Lyre of Orpheus, it is reminiscent of David and Saul in the Bible.

The symbol of the Lyra

The wings are the cerebrum, breasts of the angel, are the maxillary bodies of the fornix; the body represents the brain stem. (Ref: 109) This is the demystification of Angels playing harps.

We can also see that this symbol is close to the Arc of the Covenant, which in turn, represents the pineal and cerebrum.

(Image below taken from The Complete Anatomy App)

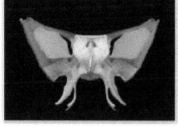

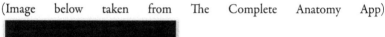

THE LAW OF LIFE IS written on Moses' stone tablets, which were stored inside the Arc of the Covenant. However, the ARC of the Covenant is also inside the head (Ref: 111). This represents the natural law stored within the DNA of each man and woman on this plane. The old covenant was the Ten Commandments, and the New Covenant is represented by the shift in consciousness when the veil was torn by Christ's sacrifice on the cross. We know this to be the ascension of the oil. The Arachnoid Mater is the web that surrounds the outer layers of the skull, also known as a veil. When one becomes illuminated, this is also pierced, as the light tears the veil between the inner and outer worlds.

The Mercy Seat

The Mercy Seat is the Sella Turcica and houses the pineal gland. It is also part of the sphenoid bone, which happens to look like an owl. The owl has always been a wise and mythical creature in all our stories and fables; now it is easy to see why this symbol means wisdom. Housing the pineal, the innerverse's aerial is an important job. This bony seat has, just like everything else, been mythologised and its true meaning forgotten. Christians take all this literally and tell you all about a seat in the tabernacle, the holy of holies, which is built along the lines of the temple as written in Exodus twenty-five verses ten to twenty-two: (Ref: 112)

Exodus 25:20-23 The heavenly creatures should have their wings spread out above, shielding the cover with their wings. The winged heavenly creatures should face each other toward the cover's center.

21 [1]Put the gold cover on top of the chest and put the covenant document that I will give you inside the chest.

22 [2]There I will meet with you. From there above the cover, from between the two winged heavenly creatures that are on top of the chest containing the covenant, I will deliver to you all that I command you concerning the Israelites.

All the pomp and ceremony of the churches showing off their ignorance to our faces. The mirrors of the inner sanctum, disrespected and diminished by their display of ungodly, hypocritical behaviour. There they all are, virtue signalling in their robes, those priests, standing on platforms, raising themselves up above everyone else, misguiding the seeker to look outside of

---

1. https://www.biblestudytools.com/ceba/exodus/25-21.html

2. https://www.biblestudytools.com/ceba/exodus/25-22.html

themselves, never encouraging them to see that the whole Bible is a book about who and what we are from our physiology to the anatomy of our spirit INSIDE. Year after year the same people sit in the same pews, the Pentecostals clapping and singing in tongues, never realising the healing they externally seek is within them, bowing and scraping to the furious God of Revelation, enthralled by skinny-jean worship-stars with no good teaching on how to really clean up the temple, filled with judgement and gossip, jostling for position in the church, hurting the true prophets, misguiding simple souls, never wanting their status, or position as a pastor or an elder to be threatened by those who may truly 'have a word' from the Godhead. How do I know? I have been there. Shut up, shut down and shut out by the cult of Christianity and frankly, it's the best thing that could have ever happened.

We are multi-dimensional instruments singing our unique blood-song. How we play our own instrument unfolds outwardly as the story of our internal lives in motion. Learning to play is the key to a happy and fulfilled life, in harmony with ourselves and others around us.

To play, just like dolphins, which remember, represent the third ventricle of the brain. To play is Leela (or Lila) in Hinduism and is their way of describing all reality, including the cosmos, as a result of the Divine Absolute's creative play. It makes sense.

As I allow my mind to be free from its conditioning, I see the beauty of all that we are. Even as I watch my own limitations and foibles express themselves, beyond the self, there is a calm, aquamarine ocean of love and gratitude. As I uncover more of who and what we are, I stand in awe over and over again. I look at the

Crista Galli (Ref: 112) and how this is attached to the Foramen and the sphenoid bone, the names are swirling around my head like mythical creatures, telling ancient stories of unicorns, sea-monsters, Owls and Sages, and sacred knowledge hidden within.

In three dimensions, all we have to go on aside from our inner knowing are the myths, stories, legends, and symbols that remind us that we are so much more than we think we know consciously. From Ancient Greece to the temples of Tibet, the truth is written on the walls of time for us to decipher. I'm taken to a beautiful Joni Mitchell song saying we are stardust and a million-year-old-carbon. We are photons, stars, and Galaxies and it is all inside our head. Eden, as I said at the beginning of the book, is inside our heads.

The land of Nod

Let us for a moment consider the Land of Nod. I feel sure that many parents have told their children they will soon be in the Land of Nod, that imaginary place of slumber.

In the book of Genesis chapter four, verse fourteen, the Land of Nod is to the east of Eden, where Cain killed his brother Abel. We know that the Garden of Eden is inside our head, therefore we can deduce the land to the East of Eden would also be there. I postulate that the land of Nod is the left hemisphere of the brain, where Cain killed Abel and the right side of the brain is the place that opens up at the point of Ascension, which may be a lifetime's work or a momentary illumination depending on the Being and their unique expression of the Godhead. (Literally.)

The left brain is generally considered to be more logical, analytical, fact-orientated, and numerical whereas the right side is more free thinking, creative, intuitive, and visual.

It could be said that Cain killing Abel represents the analytical brain, the logical left side overpowering the creative, intuitive right side, terminating the free-thinking spiritual hemisphere, a fall from grace, perhaps? (Ref: 102)

The two brothers, Cain and Abel, both made sacrifices to God, but Abel's were more pleasing causing jealousy in Cain.

And Cain said to Abel his brother, "Let us go out to the field," and when they were in the field Cain rose against Abel his brother and killed him. [iv]3 And the Lord said to Cain, "Where is Abel your brother? And he said, "I do not know: am I my brother's keeper?" [v]4 And He said, "What have you done? Listen! Your brother's blood cries out to me from the soil. And so, cursed shall you be by the soil that gaped with its mouth to take your brother's blood from your hand. If you till the soil, it will no longer give you strength. A restless wanderer shall you be on the earth." And Cain said to the Lord, "My punishment is too great to bear. Now that You have driven me this day from the soil I must hide from Your presence, I shall be a restless wanderer on the earth and whoever finds me will kill me." And the Lord said to him, "Therefore whoever kills Cain shall suffer sevenfold vengeance." And the Lord set a mark upon Cain so that whoever found him would not slay him.

---

3. https://en.wikipedia.org/wiki/Cain_and_Abel%2523cite_note-8

4. https://en.wikipedia.org/wiki/Cain_and_Abel%2523cite_note-9

And Cain went out from the Lord's presence and dwelled in the land of Nod east of Eden. And Cain knew his wife and she conceived and bore Enoch. Then he became the builder of a city and he called the name of the city like his son's name, Enoch.

The story of Cain and Abel also appears in the Koran. (Ref: 104) The definition of the Hebrew word Nod means wandering, or nomadic, which I find remarkably interesting as the Middle East if full of nomadic tribes. This, in my view, is a perfect manifestation of all that happens inside the head in the physical realm.

The right and the left hemispheres of the brain need to be in balance for an individual to have a healthy relationship with the seen and the unseen in this dimension. It could be said that Cain hiding from God's presence represents being solely left-brain orientated. All logic and no creativity. However, I postulate that when Cain met his wife (the Divine feminine) and gave birth to Enoch, He once again, as it says in the scriptures, was able to walk with God. It could be said that this is a template for humanity and our inner growth, by balancing the left and the right brain,

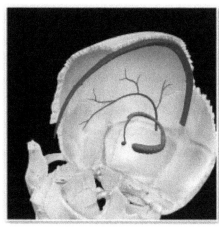

the divine masculine and feminine within.

And speaking of heads, let us examine the Superior Sagittal Sinus (thank you Ashley from China): This is the large blue vein in the picture. The smaller vein is the inferior Sagittal sinus. Why call it Sagittal? Who named it? Of course, we are reminded of the Bow of the Sagittarius Constellation.

Imagine if you will, the position of the stars at your birth and their geometrical angles in relation to where you are in the physical. Imagine that each angle creates a resonance (as it does in the physical world) and as you move and grow and change, the resonance changes frequency or tone, creating harmony or dissonance within you. The angles are "angels," geometric messengers of light, anthropomorphically represented as winged beings. The light is photons and travels as sound or frequency and is received by our antenna — the Fornix or Ammon's Horn. Sound is the carrier wave for light, consciousness, and intention. It works both ways around, from us to the universe and back.

The light issues from the universe, every planet, constellation, and beyond, and is received according to our capacity and ability. We, as co creators, beam our messages back on every level into the universe on every plane.

This thought, if truly realised, will empower and ignite us.

From the twelve Apostles (twelve cranial nerves) to the twenty-four elders (the cranial nerves come in pairs) in scripture, it is possible to see that all the stories, myths, and legends are telling us how our brain, mind, body, and soul is wired.

Without going into the function of each and every part of the body (I'd have to go back to school or find a clever clogs), I can see that in every scripture in the Bible, in the Vedas, and most so-called Holy Books, the texts are referring to the way that God moves through the physical world into manifestation. The brain itself has been personified into elephants (Ganesh), owls (sphenoid bone), pine cones (pineal), Kali (anus), and many more interesting deities and creatures. It's like a secret science told in parable form.

(See image video reference 114.)

We're not what we have been told we are. We are heavenly dragonfish, prisms of light and sound, elements and galactic symphonies, infinity itself manifesting into and out of myriad forms as consciousness raises and lowers its vibration; sometimes in harmony with itself, sometimes in dissonance but always reconciling to itself eventually.

Now, as we see our infinite potential, as we beam our lights into the earth and up into the stratosphere, we know that the darkness is not to be feared. We shine into the darkness and recover the treasures that lie waiting there. Waiting for us to pick them up and treasure them: The treasures of the innerverse.

Excerpt of a Session with Vinny M Grant:

"We're in this quantum space, a place where all things can be changed. Where the quantum selves just line up. Shapes, moving, representing the transformation of my journey. In this place, it's nothingness, the void. In this place you can change your DNA and change your blueprint to get an upgrade and activation. A place where you can be still. It's outside of everything and it's here that you can make the changes. Something in my solar plexus and in my energy field is being reconfigured. There's light in the neurones. I am seeing a massive amount of DNA, like a waterfall, twisting and turning. It's not a mental construct, something is happening to it.

"Divine intelligence within me is telling me that I am not alone. Something is coming through me in the void. All the stuff I have been holding onto is being reconfigured in a purifying fire.

"I'm standing in the middle of the wheel of life. Just standing. I just exist. I am. No more lifetimes are necessary to realise that I am. It is infinite ... indescribable. Even speaking it is a contradiction. It's beyond the mind and any conception, any images, or thoughts, beyond the beyond and it's infinite and always here. It's like grace.

"All the bad things that have happened to me were there to teach me how to love. To know that love permeates everything regardless. It's just this infinite love that permeates everything. It goes through everything. There is nothing that love can't penetrate. Love penetrates everything. There's no element that can exist without there being love in it. It is the most potent force in creation; it's the most potent energy, force, is-ness, everything. It can be a hard task master because there is no fear in love, so therefore we can't be afraid of anything. When we are feeling love, everything is possible down to an atomic level. Everything that comes into existence is because of love. God is love. Love is God."

Chapter 8

The Sympathetic Resonance of the Music of the Heart

———

Love is the Key to Life.

══════════

I'D LIKE TO START THIS chapter with a song I wrote about twenty years ago:

The Key

———

I know, we're unconventional

But love isn't something you can justify or measure

It's sensational, inspirational.

No money can buy these feelings we have inside.

And without it, we are shells

Washed up on a beach somewhere

With no-one to care for

Alone in the sand, with all the other grains of sand

Waiting for a wave to take the loneliness away

And I know

It's unmentionable, impossible to talk about

yet life is what it's all about

It's indescribable, undeniable....

No concepts can deceive it, confine it or perceive it

because love,

Love is the only way, and we don't know what it is, only what it's not and love...

Love is the Key to Life.

Without love, we are nothing. It's the strongest, most potent force in the universe. God is love, love is God. When you really get that, then all things are possible through love. Love permeates the deepest parts of the inner-verse, the multiverse, and in fact, it could be said, is creation itself. In scriptures it clearly states:

"If I speak in the tongues a of men or of angels, but do not have love, I am only a resounding gong or a clanging cymbal. 2If I have the gift of prophecy and can fathom all mysteries and all knowledge, and if I have a faith that can move mountains, but do not have love, I am nothing. 3If I give all I possess to the poor and give over my body to hardship that I may boast, b but do not have love, I gain nothing." (Ref: 115)

Life is beautiful; however, it can be extremely challenging. I know this first-hand, second-hand, and third! The only thing that has kept me going is the love I feel inside of me. Even in my darkest days (and there have been many) when I've been battling to survive or drowning in tears... the wonder of creation, the beauty of a stranger's smile, the kiss of my child, the sound of my favourite song, falling upward into a starry African sky, life is too extraordinary, too wonderful, too incredible not to love it.

The pain of love serves to awaken the slumbering soul. The pain of child birth, the pain of a traumatic childhood, the pain of losing a loved one, the end of a love affair, the torture inflicted by others, the curses, the poverty, the restless and sleepless nights, the betrayal, the abuse, the endless tears, the loneliness, the pain of separation, bad health, suffering and on and on... all of it serves an incredible purpose and that, is to wake us up to who we really are and to activate the love within us. By activating the heart, it allows the lower energies to transform into the frequency of love. Love is the key to a beautiful life.

"4Love is patient, love is kind. It does not envy, it does not boast, it is not proud. 5It does not dishonour others, it is not self-seeking, it is not easily angered, it keeps no record of wrongs. 6Love does not delight in evil but rejoices with the truth. 7It always protects, always trusts, always hopes, always perseveres." (Ref: 1 Corinthians 13:4-8)

However, pain is an essential function of life. It is another frequency and also acts as a key to unlock stubborn and sleeping hearts. The key is a musical key, a note, a tone, a frequency, and an energy.

"The heart generates a powerful electromagnetic field. When the electromagnetic field of the heart was measured on an electrocardiogram (ECG), it was found that it was about sixty times greater in amplitude than the brain waves recorded in an electroencephalogram (EEC). The electromagnetic field of the heart is so powerful that it can be measured several feet away from an individual's body."

"An electric field forms around any electric charge." (Ref: Becker, 1985) The potential difference between two points produces an electric field represented by electric lines of flux. The negative pole always has more electrons than the positive pole."

Bearing in mind that our cells make up everything in our bodies (including our hearts) and that they create their own magnetic field, it stands to reason as they are crystalline structures, that they would act as receivers and transmitters of energy and vibration. In the same way that energy is electrically stored in the magnetic field I postulate that it's the same for organic life forms. I propose that all the data, memories, and trauma etc. is stored in the magnetic field as energy, which either raises or lowers the voltage and vibration of a being. It's like musical harmony or dissonance. I knew this at age seventeen but spent a lifetime experiencing too many dissonant frequencies, transforming the energy as a singer and musician by writing positive harmonic music to unconsciously find the balance and release. My songs were a response to pain, lyrically always searching for the inner answers and melodically expressing it all through musical intervals and modulations but never succeeding in getting there until I awakened.

The sympathetic resonance of the music of the heart is totally astounding. When we sing together, our heartbeats synchronise. The same thing happens when we make love, make war, or make peace. Combining this with the fact that sound creates form (Hans Jenny) and is a carrier wave for consciousness and intention, we can join the dots together and begin to get the picture of who and what we are in manifestation.

If we examine the anatomy of intentions, we can innerstand that faith has a frequency, as does every quality, thought, or emotion. Everything is vibrating, isn't it? Our hearts beat faster when we think of something exciting or remember a trauma. How many people are replaying traumas over and over in their mind, constantly recreating the same pain over and over again, perpetuating a broken heart until it becomes chronic?

The human heartbeat changes according to the rhythm of the music you are listening to. This is why we can feel moved by a piece of music — it's because we literally are. This is known as sympathetic resonance.

"Sympathetic resonance or sympathetic vibration is a harmonic phenomenon wherein a passive string or vibratory body responds to external vibrations to which it has a harmonic likeness.[1] The classic example is demonstrated with two similarly tuned tuning forks. When one fork is struck and held near the other, vibrations are induced in the un-struck fork, even though there is no physical contact between them."

For example, if you have twenty-five grand pianos in a hall, put down the sustain peddle on all of them and play a note on one, they will all start resonating at the same note or frequency. We as organic beings do exactly the same thing, and it could be said that this is a perfect example of thoughts and emotions. From sympathy to hilarity, thoughts and emotions are exchanged energetically and deeply felt between people consciously, subconsciously, or, rebuked, rebutted, and rejected. This can all be held or stored in the electromagnetic field around our body. These frequencies are contagious and transforming, received, or rejected. Comprehending how electricity, voltage, and vibration work will empower us to transcend our dissonance.

When I was young, I remember having relationships with men and noticing how closed their hearts were. Young men with closed hearts. As time passed and I never found the one, my own heart grew numb, leaving me unable to trust (no oxytocin), or believe in love.

Resonance behaviour causes mirror neurones to mimic whatever we focus our attention on. Ninety-eight percent of our neurones will be firing in precisely the same way as whatever we are paying attention to, leaving only two percent of us with our own feelings or neurological programming.

But as stated above, the heart creates a powerful electromagnetic field:

"Sixty times greater in amplitude than the brain waves recorded in an electroencephalogram" and yet we ignore the heart, preferring to lend credence to the brain.

The heart is a robust piece of kit but can literally be broken or lacerated through stress or loss — especially of loved ones. Just like the hippocampus can be physically scarred, so can our hearts. We need to examine our hearts first and then our heads.

In scripture it says:

9 The heart is deceitful above all things, and desperately sick; who can understand it? 10 "I the Lord search the heart and test the mind, to give every man according to his ways, according to the fruit of his deeds." (Jeremiah 17:9-10)

This *scripture* is deceptive. The heart is a beautiful organ and cannot be deceptive and yet the Bible bashers would take this literally and preach you into guilt, submission, and worthlessness. The mind, however, can be programmed to be deceptive, which can negatively affect the heart, of course.

The being presents as deceptive if the heart is not in alignment or functioning properly. When people experience trauma and it is stuck in their electromagnetic field, everything is skewed. Perception is warped. Should the person be in emotional pain or confusion, of course this will manifest as sickness, but it's not the heart, is it? It is the dissonance, the enharmonic energy personified or embodied.

What this really means is what you give is what you get, over lifetimes, not just this one. The hearts of our ancestors play a big part in our predisposition. When we awaken, we reposition and deposition.

Also, research suggests that sex is good for a healthy heart and decreases the likelihood of heart attacks by creating oxytocin, which, once released into the blood can have incredible effects such as building trust, healing wounds both physically, mentally, and emotionally, and reducing stress. Good lovemaking or sex can also stimulate adrenaline and endorphins, which act as a natural painkiller, plus serotonin, which creates a feeling of wellbeing or happiness. When you laugh, there is a twenty percent increase in blood flow from the heart so the cure would be plenty of good lovemaking and a lot of laughter. Sounds like fun to me.

"When was the last time you had any REAL FUN?" a friend inquired. "Fun is a spiritual value." It took a while to let that land.

If only life were that simple. Well, it is. We just make it overly complicated owing to a lack of innerstanding, being disconnected from our hearts, and therefore sending out dissonance instead of harmony into the field.

I realised recently that I was being guided to write this chapter for my own learning. I am reminded that when I was in my twenties, I would visualise something and sure enough it would happen soon afterwards in a matter of weeks. So why in my fifties is it so much more challenging? Why?

Aside from the incredible mess on planet Earth at the moment, it is about this heart connection. I would say that it's impossible to break through all the thick vibrations that are issuing into the atmosphere, like some kind of boil bursting, without maintaining a strong heart connection to oneself and each other.

The events since the end of December 2019 have on the one hand divided people, caused pain, misery, and death, and on the other, profoundly re-awakened enormous amounts of people to the truth about themselves, the world, and their reality from their straw man and fiat currency to spirituality, so-called ascension, and our expanding consciousness.

Never have so many conspiracy theorists, sooth-sayers, astrologers, alien worshippers, and yoga freaks been so busy, all claiming their truth.

"The aliens are coming!"

"Operation Blue-beam is going to fake it!"

"It's the great awakening!"

"It's revelation and the end times!"

And on it goes. On a daily basis, these words are spoken into being, into this reality, as a self-fulfilling prophecy.

The Revelation, is within, and it is not intellectual. It is energetic.

The realisation is that without love we are nothing and in order to love we NEED to forgive both ourselves and EVERYBODY for being "hu"man and contaminated by the frequencies (hues) of this planet as it's going through this huge change. None of us can cast a stone in judgement of another. We have all been part of this timeline over and over again and need to take response-ability for all of it, starting with ourselves by examining our own hearts. (N.B: one definition for the word Hu is God or Spirit.)

Working from a broken to an awakened heart is the key. The key is the frequency, and the frequency is the musical note caused by the resonance (or dissonance), which in turn is literally caused by the shape of something. For example, the resonant frequency of a room is denoted by its shape. Therefore, the geometry of the heart is the true frequency, and the healing takes place internally and externally as we tune in, examine ourselves honestly and then, through waking up to ourselves, let the process happen. This means we might need to face all the bits about ourselves that are not so fabulous. But we need to do so without any condemnation or judgement.

Condemnation is a trap that recycles old beliefs and notions in a pot of repetition, served up over and over on a daily basis until we change the recipe.

Bearing in mind that our hearts are sixty times greater in amplitude than our brains, it stands to reason that if we are nursing a dissonance, or walking around with a broken heart, the rest of our being will not be functioning properly.

It's only now that I realised that my heart has been broken for years. The reason I have attracted more of the same stuff over and over is because I've never healed my brokenness. The question is, how can you mend a broken heart? How indeed...?

Personally speaking, I have learnt that gratitude is my first port of call. I have had so much to be grateful for. I mean sometimes, when the muck hit the fan and I was standing in front of it, it was hard to find something to be thankful for, but there was ALWAYS something. Always.

Being thankful for another breath is what it came down to at one point, having nearly died with acute pancreatitis. I had to make the decision: "Do I want to carry on or not?"

When you feel like you are suspended in emotional formaldehyde, it can be a challenge to continue, knowing that it is YOU who needs to change. Acting like a Damian Hurst sawn cow on display for all to see (this artist's work, including the cows, can be seen in London's Tate Gallery) creates drama resulting in the Christmas card list having only one or two people left on it ... if you're lucky.

So why have a Bible at all? Why have scripts and Holy Books if the meanings are lost and the stories are taken literally, played out as a self-fulfilling prophecy and an excuse for bad behaviour? What is the point of it when we have so-called science to tell us what things are and how they work? Is it all just a load of superstitious nonsense?

Interestingly, the science we have today is somewhat up its own backside. In school we get half-truths with no practical applications or comprehension of how the Ancients, for example Pythagoras, calculated such complicated equations. Instead, we are examined on how much we can remember of other people's thinking without truly knowing the meaning. Hence geometry is not sacred, hormones are not understood, gender is now a free-for-all, and the sheep have no idea whether they are rams or ewes. As for the shepherds, you have to wonder how they got the job in the first place.

We have half the story in science and the other half in spiritual practices. Bringing the two together will create such a shift in consciousness that we will never look back to these dark days of superstition and ignorance.

Comprehending what we have come to term as Spirit is essential in order for science to progress. It could be said that spirit is energy and vibration and that the new term for it is Quantum physics, quantum alchemy, and so on. However, this is just the doorway to comprehending the infinite. Without a good foundation, we would be lost or chasing our own tail very quickly.

Over the past few centuries, we have become so incredibly dumb and inept at critical, deep thinking and discerning the unseen, opting for external distraction and hedonism to the extreme. Now, with all this talk of ascension, we may need to actually clean up our act before we rise to a higher state of being or it could be a very painful process indeed.

Imagine an education system that included quantum alchemy, sacred geometry, a period table for spiritual elements, physiology, and a creative psychology, and which allowed a child to think for themselves and not be examined on other people's restrictive beliefs based on cruel experiments performed on poorer classes. Imagine what kind of kids we would have and what kind of future they would build.

How about a world where Satan was innerstood as the energy of Saturn and could be quantified in such a way that was relevant to how this energy moved in our own resonant map.

Imagine demystifying Baphomet, its symbol and taking out all that mental aberration, trauma, and distortion and dumping it in the trash, where it belongs. Once and for all. All we need to do is see the wizard behind the curtain for who and what he is. Ready?

Baphomet:

(See image: Ref 116)

Here we have a lot of ignorance and so-called dirty secrets to blast through. What a lot of spiritual excrement has been heaped upon this symbol. It is such a distortion that one needs to put on spiritual headphones or noise blockers.

Humans do love a good story, and for some reason, the more dangerous the better. Most of the current adventure movies thrive on blood and guts being spilled everywhere from savage killings to fierce battles, to interdimensional power struggles. I personally cannot watch the endless killing and maiming of creatures, no matter which imagination they spring from. I would rather watch something uplifting. However, that old entrainment program starts from conception and is perpetuated by the endless, fearful narrative that emanates through every channel it can. Knowing is a powerful weapon.

Whether it is the symbols used for the Christ, for Ganesh, Vishnu, or Baphomet, the root is always the same. Whether it has been encrypted by the Abash Cipher or worshipped by a demonic cult, the origins are always the same. The answer is literally inside of us.

The process of storytelling to illustrate a point is fascinating but seems to have got a little bit out of hand in recent decades. Stories of demons, entities anthropomorphically represented are, when examined, only three-dimensional ways of expressing energies unseen to slumbering eyes whose attention is easily distracted and funnelled into an illusion, which leads on to more illusion.

I have seen, heard, and experienced these entities when dealing with people (including myself) who needed deliverance. I myself was released from what can only be described as a horned beast with wings and claws that was trying to strangle me and stop me from saying "Jesus Christ is my Lord and Saviour," as I took myself through a freedom from freemasonry course. So what are these things?

It could be said that something from another dimension (let us assume it is of a higher vibration) entering the third dimension would be somewhat restricted in appearance. We may see it as a sphere, but it could be a hepteract, and, just as we see a sphere, something in two dimensions would perceive it as a disc or flat circle. In my humble opinion, we have been trained not to see.

Looking at Baphomet, by stripping away the human stories, the idol worship, and in this case dreadful imagination, we see, yet again, a direct correlation to the brain stem. We see wings (Cerebrum), arms (Brachium of inferior colliculus) a face, horns, legs, and so on. (Please view Reference 116.) We also see that this part of the brain and body has been completely demonised. It is the same brain stem. The same body part that is symbolised by Jesus hanging on the cross. Personally, I think we are ready now to innerstand what and who we are, and the incredible functions of every part of the body, on every level and in every dimension. Is it not about time we stopped the nonsense? Or does someone still believe in Santa Claus and not the scientifically proven story of the claustrum?

In electronics, the colour red symbolises a live current. Knowing we are electric beings, with this in mind, notice the colour red used in most Baphomet symbols at the base. Notice that the energy is moving upward through the caduceus symbol (the two snakes) toward the centre, which is the superior antillery vellum. The breasts represent the superior colliculus. The face itself represents the pineal gland. The fire issuing from the top of the head represents the internal fire or energy enlightening the pineal and raising up through the third ventricle, to the fornix (furnace), where connection with the divine is ignited, enlightening the crown energy centre. The five-pointed star is used and needs careful examination.

The Pentagram

The Pentagram was used by the Mesopotamians as far back as three and a half thousand years ago. Wiccans, Early Christians, and now the Church of Latter-Day Saints, Pythagoreans, Alchemists, Pagans, Hebrews, Catholics, the Ancient Chinese and Japanese, Mathematicians, and Satanists all use this symbol for different purposes, which speaks volumes about its power. Whether it symbolises the five elements, harmony and spirituality, feminine energy, a spell-casting tool, protection or reversed (all that is anti the above) it is sacred geometry. It creates a harmonic resonance or discord depending on the intention of its user and position in space.

Just as we have a comprehension of physical circuitry, there is an invisible world with circuits, rules, resonances, vibrations, causes, and effects. As energy transforms throughout the multiverse through angles and geometric shapes into what we know as space that invisible world manifests.

The word Baphomet has a number of different origins and uses.

Here is a list of a few of them:

· Bafumarias — old name for Islamic Mosques or Temples in around 1090

· Mahommet — old French corruption of the word Mohamed

· Knights Templars accused of worshipping Arabian idol Baphomet in approximately 1090

· Abu Fihamat — Arabic word meaning The Father of Understanding

· Sophia — the encrypted word for Baphomet (using the Atbash Cipher — Reference 117), which means knowledge or wisdom or Goddess. (Greek)

· Occult practices, including the Kabbalah, use this symbol for illusory things that I shall not mention here.

Baphomet (or Sophia, which is Greek for Wisdom) is an anthropomorphic symbol of the brain that includes the incredible vagus nerve. The Ancient stories about it are all very similar and all point to an awakening or becoming conscious through the purging of sin. Nothing more and nothing less. All this nonsense of devil worship and unseen entities is a human way of perceiving unseen dimensions (literally geometric frequencies) and intentions. At its best it is wisdom, truth, love, and eternal values. Reversed it is ignorance, evil intentions, and negative energy. It is time to raise ourselves out of the mud and educate each other, each filling in the missing pieces.

The vagus nerve plays an important role in our daily function and forms part of the symbol of the crucifix. All the old symbols of Gods and Goddesses, Kings and Queens represent our bodies, our brains, our arteries, veins, neurological, and hormonal systems. My favourite representation is Ganesh, who, it could be said, opened the door to this new way of seeing things. I've always liked elephants and now I comprehend why. (Ref: 126)

Chapter 9

Recovering the Hidden Treasures of Darkness

───
───

───────
───────

ISAIAH 45:3 "AND I will give you the treasures of darkness, and hidden riches of secret places, that you may know that I, the lord, which call you by your name, even (am) the God of Israel."

Translated: I will give you the inner wisdom and hidden internal secrets so that we may know each other intimately in the same way as I call the 'God of Israel'. (The definition of Is - ra - el means struggle with God.)

"Who calls you by name" translates into sonic frequency. We each and every one of us has a unique resonance; just like our thumb prints, there are no two alike. This is science fact. (Ref: 118)

Recovering hidden treasure alludes to something having been stolen or taken away, something that belongs to you, that is inherently yours. Regardless of how this may have happened (and there are many theories out there and some of them are very way out there) the point is to start the recovery process.

This text is said to have been written by a prophet (Isaiah) 800 years BC. We don't know if this is true, but the point is that something has been taken and someone (or thing) is calling us back to ourselves. It could be said that we are calling ourselves back (not that there is such a thing as direction ultimately) to who we truly are. The only way to do it is by returning to the inner worlds. The reason I say this is because in Genesis, creator is plural:

"Then God said, "Let us make mankind in our image, in our likeness, so that they may rule over the fish in the sea and the birds in the sky, over the livestock and all the wild animals, and over all the creatures that move along the ground." (Ref: 119)

The word Isaiah means "salvation of Yahwey."

Salvation means to bring to safety or rescue from danger.

Yahweh means I am.

Salve means healing ointment. One can deduce the meaning from the above: The salvation of "I am."

The book of Isaiah is all about healing, rescuing from danger (or misalignment/spiritual dissonance) and applying the salve or balm of the deeper connection with creator. Big clue in the name: Both the Old Testament and the New tell the same story of salvation in a hundred different ways, as do the Holy Books of the East (Gita, Book of the Dead, etc.).

In our current global spiritual climate, there is much deception and apparent three-dimensional thievery. This makes the natural inhabitants of this plane(t) suffer as a consequence — mainly through lack of knowledge of how to live and why we are here. From the notions of quantum holographic realities to operation blue-beam, the souls of people are entrapped in a prison of their own making as they have no idea that they are co-creating all of this. It's time to take full "response-ability" for ourselves. That literally means complete, not partial.

The salvation of I am.

(Bear in mind that the salvation is known to be the Amen.)

The healing of, from, and by the I am consciousness within each of us, is the process known as recovering the hidden treasures of darkness.

I would postulate that this is more of an uncovering of what already lies within or the shedding light upon rather than a roadside recovery. What have we lost in reality? The truth is, probably nothing because it's all there lying dormant within us. But let's look at this from a basic perspective. We've forgotten how to look.

Our governments have deceived us through the birth certificate fraud, through partial education without context, and thus disempowered our ability to reason and cognite in all areas of academia — hence restricting critical thinking. Free analytical speech now causes offence to someone, somewhere. They've poisoned our food, lied through religion, and caused wars, pain, killing, torture, famine, and poverty. They've tricked us all, but who allowed this to happen? We did.

There is no them and us. We must innerstand that we are the people who need to take a stand. As high vibrational beings we should be immune to such density. However, if our slumbering hypnosis continues, the lower currents could easily pull us down to the murky bottom of the sea bed.

Regardless of what the whole truth is (look within and you will find it) about this universe, the way out of mental and spiritual captivity, is in.

Going in through our inner portals, finding our way to the secret innerverse, which resides in an untouchable, sacred place, uniquely ours, is our individual expression of the divine.

The first diplomatic immunity is internal as we come to realise who we are as eternal beings. As a latent effect of that innerstanding, it's granted to us here on this plane through due diligence and faith. It works from the inside out. Spiritual authority comes through knowing the God within, not quoting the god without! It could be said that we are the walking, talking books of the law. The "law" is our internal system or constellation, which is inherently good and divinely created.

As we come into alignment with Creator, with source, the is that is all and all that is, our energy doesn't leak and is potentised through the eternal revelations of truth and freedom. More photons are able to pierce the darkness of ignorance and shine a light on treasures we never knew we possessed.

The gifts:

· Foresight

· Insight

· Energetic transformation

· Multidimensional awareness and consciousness The ability to clearly discern energy (spirit)

· Fortitude

· Resistance (immunity to hatred and other dissonances)

· Consistent stability or balance

· Perseverance

· Good health

· Manifestation (speaking life into being, bringing life into being)

· Healing

· Artistic expression through all mediums (from music to maths)

· Mental clarity and agility

· Transference of knowledge (the ability to teach others)

· Radiance (an open, generous, loving heart)

· Compassion

· Joy

· Wisdom

· Selflessness (no ego)

· Honesty

· Generosity

· Abundance

· Faith

· Love and love, is the key to life.

As we shine the inner light upon ourselves first, the treasures we already possess (only a few of which are named above) are revealed and recovered. I am here to remind you of who you truly are. No demonisation, no mind control, no indoctrination, just you and your hidden treasures now revealed.

As we enter the innerverse through the constellations of the heart, mind, and soul, the archetypes play out for us on our internal screen as we perceive that which is beyond personification. The innerverse and the multiverse as one, in communion through resonance, geometry and flowing photons of light and sound.

Our treasures have not been stolen; we have just forgotten we have them. Let's take this recovery as a period of time following illness. It's actually more like recuperation following our time as sleeping beauty.

Allowing our beauty to awaken is essential in order to love ourselves for who and what we truly are, regardless of the considered aesthetic.

I remember, when I was about eight years old, I had a surrogate grandmother who was about sixty-three. She was well worn, slightly tanned all year round, a spiritualist, and an artist. My mother would leave me with her regularly. I would sit in her garden, watch her paint, relax in her blanket-covered chairs, and stare out of the window whilst she shared her spiritual wisdom with me. I'd ask impossible questions and she would always try to give me an answer; if she did not know, she'd say so. I thought she was beautiful. I did not see her age or shape. To me she was kind, loving, caring, and always there for me. She was no relation but sent by the divine to school me in spiritual things. I saw her aura and felt the resonance of her heart. She never restricted me and gave me space to be free. I loved every line on her face and was fascinated by her dark eyes and curly hair. I remember looking at pictures of her as a child with her dark complexion and long, wavy, dark locks down to her bottom. Who was she? I never really knew, but to me, she was a gifted, kind, spiritual adopted Grandmother who loved me while I was there.

That memory is a treasure I will never forget. It took a while to realise it as I had to shake off the negative impressions of my narcissistic father who spouted nothing but scorn, judgement, and hatred for this woman whom he never really knew.

The process of my recovery has been long and arduous. My path has been rocky and painful. Through it all, once the dust was removed, I have reclaimed my birthright and I am breathing it in.

The treasures of my life were saturated by my tears. The constant blows punched by those whom I have loved the most, caused me to

let go of all I thought I once needed in favour of a true relationship
with what I know as God.

Chapter 10
Speaking Trees

———

———————

I HAVE ALWAYS HAD A deep connection with trees; never more so than now. To see the trees, I knew and loved so well as a child still majestically standing in the same place, nearly fifty years later, is both comforting and awe inspiring. There are two cedar trees I have admired every time I have passed since I was seven years old. On the way to my favourite beach, there are pine trees whose needles I used to collect and make things with at age five. They are still standing, stretching their beings up toward the sunlight.

In fact, there are trees to whom I feel connected all over the world and whose beauty and natural wisdom I stand in awe of. From the very first weeping willow tree I remember in our back garden at the age of two to the gnarled and awkward looking madame who told me: "It's time to wake up the trees" I now comprehend a little of their importance and magical qualities.

At this time in my life, although I live in a humble dwelling, I am surrounded by trees at the back of the house. They whisper secret things to the wind, stand between us and the grumpy neighbours, provide a resting place for the dawn's orchestra, and generate nuts for the local squirrels who jump like crazed Kamikaze from branch to branch all the way down to the bottom of the block, making us smile on days when the spirit winds are blowing a hoolie in the wrong direction.

My garden is a sow's ear but is rescued by the trees who just stand there looking beautiful for three seasons until each autumnal leaf must finally let go. I've watched their dressing and undressing for ten long years, never dreaming that I would be so connected to this tiny little piece of earth. It was only ever going to be a short stay. But during my time here, I have undergone the greatest transformation I could ever have asked for, losing everything I thought I had until I realised it was never mine and until I realised that all I have and will ever have is within me.

Oh yes, I knew this when I was young, like we all do. It was easy then because there was nothing to hold on to and no reason to either. Then, when the indoctrination began in earnest from the age of seven, the internal rebellion began. Now, when you are awake to all lifetimes, awake to the lies, awake to the deception and try to live within it, it's a living hell. That was my childhood. My childhood seemed to last for an extremely long time until all family passed away until finally, yes finally, the spiritual suckers draining me of my life-force were cut once and for all. Harsh words but true. I am grateful for it all, because if it had not been for the pain, I would not have had to dig deep to find my one true connection with that which created me.

Now, let's get it straight, my connection and expression of divinity is totally unique — as is yours — and that's the point and the beauty of it all. There is no judgement in how this is expressed. Our DNA is our love-song to God and the universe, our true name, our calling, signal to others, our unique frequency. I postulate that this unique vibration (or call sign for Ham radio enthusiasts) is what the natural world responds to, from our pets to the trees. In fact, I know that my pets can hear me coming from a few miles away and come to the door or the window (my family tell me) and wait, ready for their hugs when I get home. It's my belief that they vibrate on the frequency of love and don't comprehend cruelty or dissonance. Some pets resonate on the frequency of food, but that's another story.

In my experience, it's the animals and plants in my life who have taught me how to love, as they seem to do it so unconditionally. They are such incredible creatures who just know. I am so grateful for my feline friends who have seen me through more turbulence than all my human friends. My beloved Percy, Yetti, and Salome who lasted the best part of twenty years, followed shortly after by Teddy and Thursday, who were with me for another twenty years. Teddy died in 2020 at the age of twenty. For the full story, please see Reference 120.

In my life, I have failed on so many occasions to truly love and let go. That is, until I gave birth to the love of my life, who has been the greatest teacher of all. I have loved and lost so many times as the rebelliousness in me rears its Samurai head. I cannot comprehend conformity, lies, abuse, selfishness, and a lack of respect from men to women. I have had many lessons to learn in this area and feel like a Lion these days if someone is dishonest, refuses to take responsibility, or is disrespectful. I tend to roar. Perhaps my love of feline companions rubbed off? Perhaps I come across too strongly as I patrol my new-found boundaries.

This year I have planted four trees and have two more to place. They have given me apples and cherries already. Each time I look at them I smile in wonder, as they adjust to the change of the seasons and grow into themselves. I smile in awe of my own child who is growing into a beautiful, majestic tree, mighty and strong, already bearing much fruit.

I am reminded that "tree" was an old name for *people* in ancient Hebrew. There are many English idioms regarding trees, particularly oaks, for example:

· "Mighty oaks from little acorns grow"

· "He's a good oak,"

· "As strong as an oak..." etc., etc.

There really is a lot to say about trees and their essential part in sustaining life here on this plane. They are such mystical beings and long to be talked to and loved just like we do.

Druids, Shamans, Healers, Wiccans, Wizards, children, and all those who are awakened talk to trees. There are so many beautiful stories about these ancient ones who hold up the sky.

The Kalpavriksha (Kalpa) tree is known as the wishing tree in Indian mythology. It is prayed to directly, as it is believed to have a connection to the Divine.

It could be said that just as trees convert carbon dioxide into oxygen making air breathable, they take negative energy or dissonance and transform it back into harmonic frequencies. Think about it, their function is not just for the physical realm, it is on every level of consciousness.

"Yggdrasill, Old Norse Mimameidr, in Norse mythology, the world tree[1] is a giant ash supporting the universe. One of its roots extended into Niflheim[2]*, the underworld; another into Jötunheim, land of the giants; and the third into Asgard[3], home of the gods.

"At its base were three wells: Urdarbrunnr (Well of Fate), from which the tree was watered by the Norns (the Fates); Hvergelmir (Roaring Kettle), in which dwelt Nidhogg, the monster that gnawed at the tree's roots; and Mímisbrunnr (Mimir's Well), source of wisdom, for the waters of which Odin sacrificed an eye.

"After Ragnarök (Doomsday), the world tree, though badly shaken, was to be the source of new life." (Ref: 121)

"Not only do they hold up the sky, but more than any other living things, trees define our sense of place and provide much needed equilibrium." (Ref: 122)

In the scripts from the Bible to the Gita, from ancient Norse to the Germanic myths, trees figure very highly. However, I'd like to invite you, once again, to look inside the structure of the human brain. (Ref: 127)

Upon reading the myths and scripts, you will see that everything correlates with the inner structures of the brain.

---

1. https://www.britannica.com/topic/world-tree

2. https://www.britannica.com/topic/Niflheim

3. https://www.britannica.com/topic/Asgard

"In the vertical, tree-of-knowledge tradition, the tree extends between earth and heaven. It is the vital connection between the world of the gods and the human world. Oracles and judgments or other prophetic activities are performed at its base. In the horizontal, tree-of-life tradition, the tree is planted at the centre of the world and is protected by supernatural guardians. It is the source of terrestrial fertility and life. Human life is descended from it; its fruit confers everlasting life; and if it were cut down, all fecundity would cease. The tree of life occurs most commonly in quest romances in which the hero seeks the tree and must overcome a variety of obstacles on his way." (Ref: 123)

From a basic structural description to the deeper spiritual functions of the mind and beyond, it could be said that the Arbor Vitae is directly comparable to the world tree in Norse and Germanic mythology, the tree of life in Genesis (Bible), the Peepal Tree in Hinduism, and the Bodhi Tree in Buddhism. In the classic image below we see the Arbor Vitae and the elephant surrounded by stars (inner constellations). The elephant (Ganesh) symbolises the medulla Oblongata (as seen in previous chapters), which is right next to the Arbor Vitae (tree of life) in the brain."The tree is planted at the centre of the world and is protected by supernatural guardians."

(Ref: Britannica, The Editors of Encyclopaedia. "world tree". Encyclopedia Britannica, 8 Nov. 2015, https://www.britannica.com/topic/world-tree. Accessed 24 February 2023.)

"The arbor vitae lies in the center of the cerebellum and is critical in the coordination of the arms, legs and any actions requiring hand-eye coordination. The arbor vitae is made of white matter that transmits information throughout the brain." (Ref: 124)

"It is made up of a tree-shaped white substance known as arbor vitae in the cerebrum. Axons contain nerves that transmit signals between the brain and spinal cord. The Latin term tree of life refers to a tree. The arbor vitae is a white matter found in the cerebrum. It is required for the proper functioning of the brain. A tree or shrub that has thin outer bark as well as fibrous inner bark is referred to as arborvitae. They grow in a way that mimics the appearance of veins and roots." (Ref: 125)

The shape of the Arbor Vitae is reminiscent of the pine tree, which of course would correlate with the pineal being the fruit of the tree. Axons are similar in function to the fungi that trees use to communicate with each other via their roots, sending electrical signals of communication through the mycelium, just like us. My postulate is that this works on an energetic level, as we all communicate with each other through the aether and our biomagnetic fields of resonance. (Ref: 127)

"Now the Tree of Life was in the middle of the garden, and also the Tree of Knowledge of Good and Evil. 10 A river flowed out of Eden to water the garden. From there it divided and became four riverheads. 11 The name of the first is Pishon, the one that winds around the whole land of the Havilah, where there is gold. 12 The gold of that land is good—bdellium and lapis lazuli stones are also there. 13 The name of the second river is Gihon—it winds around the whole land of Cush. 14 The name of the third river is Tigris—it runs east of Assyria. And the fourth river is Euphrates." (Genesis 2:9-15)

The four river heads or tributaries are the veins.

The Land of Havilah means encircle or to whirl. Land of Gold and precious stones. In the centre of Havilah is the pineal which creates the golden melatonin.

Pishon means to break apart or scatter or scatterer or disperser. Also overflowing or springing or flowing freely.

Gihon means gusher, to burst forth. "Of this river it is said that it flows around the whole land of Cush." (Genesis 2:13).

Tigris means tiger, sharper, pointed, or faster and shorter. Swift river. Euphrates means wide-flowing river, good to cross over.

Now we all know that I am not a biologist so I could be wrong about all of this and I'm prepared for that.

It might be the Jugular veins, the Superior Sagittal Sinus, Straight sinus, vein of Galen that is represented, which was my first thought; or it might be the middle cerebral artery, vertebral artery, internal carotid artery, and posterior artery in the brain. However, the point is that what we are talking about are veins, some short, some long and wide, some slow- and some fast-flowing. Without spending a year studying this to the point of complete comprehension, I am inviting you to think about this and approach what is written in the scripts from an allegorical and symbolic perspective. They all say similar things.

Remembering that the blue Gods in Hinduism symbolise the veinous system and the red Gods the arterial system, one can see that each part of the brain is artistically represented.

Creation is exquisite, as is the personification and definition in each sacred text.

One can visually see the representation of the veinous system picture of Shiva. The cobra, wrapped around the neck refers to the opening of the pineal gland. In ancient Egyptology, the cobra represented the raising of the life force (Kundalini), which would cause the pineal to light up and stand erect in the brain like a small pine tree. (Ref: 129)

In the images (Ref: 130) we have Shiva on the left and the same ancient Egyptian symbol used to represent the same thing on the right. The only way to hide the truth in plain sight is through the use of symbols. After a few weeks of researching the meaning of the Was Sceptre and Triton, I postulate (and I may be wrong) that they symbolise the third Ventricle of the Brain, where the Cerebral Spinal Fluid is created.

The spanner end of the Was sceptre looks rather like something one would place into the earth to literally ground energy. The freemasons use two spanners as part of their symbology, so whether this is an instrument of construction, a sonic device (as some would claim), or just a Set square, it's time we looked at things without trying to either demonise or fantasise about them. In the picture in the next reference, we see the deity Set. Very simply, he has the head of a strange-looking creature. Please examine Reference 130.

Notice the face and the horns of the image in the reference. Notice where the third ventricle is situated. Now look at the symbol of Set. It brings a whole new meaning to the Set square. But in all seriousness, look. It is clear to see.

The concerning thing here is the universal misrepresentation of such simple things. The lies and the mystery that have been concocted concerning who and what we are, are astounding. Imagine if we all learnt this stuff in school as part of our heritage. Imagine the effect it would have on our children and future generations.

Imagine if we innerstood that the story of Set is the story of what is going on within all of us. Transcending the lower nature as part of our growth cycle, unfolding into the divine beings we truly are.

Without going into the so-called ubiquitous meaning of the Was sceptre, I postulate that it is actually far simpler than we think. To me, it symbolises one who has mastered the body, the internal processes, and the greater mind. One who has the ability to see into the multiverse or in old money, the spiritual realms and who has been gifted with an activated brain, open loving heart, inner power, and knowledge. All the mumbo jumbo about this old sceptre and other symbols is just a distraction from the truth, which is that the Priest-Kings and Queens of the ancient world underwent a lot of spiritual training and discipline in order to earn the right to hold the rod of power and authority. They knew about the brain, mind, soul, spirit, and functions of the body. They had access to technology that has been hidden from us today. The knowledge, albeit fragmented, is written inside of us and speaks to us universally through symbols. It is just as simple as that; as I write this, sitting in suburbia, I have visions of other lifetimes and timelines where I am accessing all this knowledge and somehow, it seems that all lifetimes are one.

The new age has all but evaporated any truth and knowledge held within the hieroglyphics, scriptures, holy books, languages, and mythologies, vamping up the lower nature and adorning it as sacred in all its aberration. It is time to reclaim our birth right and know who we are from the inside out.

N.B.: When reading old texts (e.g. Hieroglyphics) remember to begin reading from right to left and then left to right. Boustrophedon seems like a much more natural way of reading and writing than the current mode.

Coming back to the Arbor Vitae inside our incredible heads, it is time to shake the tree to get the fruit and to eat it so we can be the light, be the Christ that dwells within us, and shine. Through our resonance, we will OUT shine those who would try with all their might to enslave us either through thought, word, or deed or indeed the sonic weaponry that seems to be coming to the fore.

It is my belief that we are all connected through resonance, light and sound. Just like the mycelium that trees use to communicate, our brains do exactly the same thing, sending thought waves, electrical pulses from the innerverse to the outer-verse and all multiverses as a quantum radio wave. The external reality is the latent effect, remember, and just like a battery stores excess energy in its field, we store the so-called unconscious mind, or long-term memories, including all ancestral patterns, DNA, genetic memories, and lifetimes we have all lived and re-lived. It is my belief that trees are so much a part of us and our consciousness.

In my humble opinion, just like every other being or resonant frequency on the planet, the tree holds the lifespan of its own infinite history in its electromagnetic field. Perhaps, as well, for every human tree of life, there is an external manifestation planted into the earth and they long to communicate with us, long to help us, impart their wisdom, and whisper truths when the wind shakes their leaves.

For every plant, insect, bird, and living thing, it is all an outer expression of our inner selves.

We need to be kind and respectful to all living things, which of course, we are not. Every time we treat something in the external world with disrespect, we are doing it to ourselves. There is no getting away from it.

Even the spider has its place.

"The arachnoid mater (or simply arachnoid) is one of the three meninges, the protective membranes that cover the brain and spinal cord. It is so named because of its resemblance to a spider web. The arachnoid mater is a derivative of the neural crest mesectoderm in the embryo."

Arachnoid definition — spider (Greek) Mater definition — Mother

In a recent session with Vinny M Grant, I found myself disentagling from an enormous web which covered the whole planet. I could see many people doing the same thing as me at the same time. It was as though we were all coming into consciousness and out of illusion en masse. In sync with my friend and editor of this book (Tonya Cannariato) more about the spider and arachnoid mater has been revealed. As a published author, incredible empath, intuitive, general clever-clogs and animal whisperer, her insight is extremely valuable.

Tonya Cannariato: "Remember that spider is the keeper of the knowledge of the primordial alphabet. Spider can teach how to use the written language with power and creativity so that your words weave a web around those who would read them." The important thing then for humans who are looking to break out of the arachnoid mater of their spiritual traditions' stories is that they have that same alphabet within themselves. They can write a more powerful story than what has been obfuscated by tradition, myth, and doctrine by simply understanding the truths revealed in this book."

.According to Hindu tradition, the Spider is the weaver of illusion or maya. The spider is called Arachne in Greek mythology and her story is a warning about hubris following her weaving a perfect tapestry as a challenge to Minnerva, goddess of wisdom and crafts. She is found in the Scandinavian folk lore as the women who weave, cut and measure the threads of life. In native American traditions, she is grandmother spider, the master weaver who links the past and the future, teaching the mysteries of the past and how they affect the future. From my viewpoint, I saw how this weaving was holding everything in place through the frequency of ideas, gemoetric shapes and energy manifested as the outplaying of our life story, which, like the weaver of the silken thread herself, takes great precision and agility to balance upon and connect the pieces together. The spider reminds us that we are the centre of all we weave as we create our own destiny; spinning our reality into being, and then, breaking through the illusion of matter into a wider expansion of consciousness.

Sexuality

As a woman (and not the new Cambridge definition of one) my energy is unique and I bear gifts that only women can. As women, whether we give birth or not, our feminine energy is sacred and a grace to the man. Our female organs are the reflection of all that is above the heart. The glottis and vocal cords represent the vagina, the jaw represents the hips, the intestine represents the brain, the pituitary is the hypodermis and the pineal, the G-spot. It sheds a whole new light on mind-blowing sex and lovemaking. The best thing to do here is consult the Kama Sutra or similar for more information on how to achieve the best results your body can provide.

Knowing we are energy and frequency manifesting through a body, we have to ask ourselves: "What is our true intention?" (The anatomy of intention is a frequency or sonic resonance that vibrates according to the type of thought you are emitting. i.e. sound is a carrier wave for intention.)

There are many who use sex and the power of the lower energy centres for their own personal gain. To have control over others, to subdue, hurt or dominate through the misuse of this sexual energy. It is very low in vibration and is a thirst that remains unquenched. Debauchery, addiction, and lust can become the predominant forces that lead people into a pit of despair and deviance and a loveless state of being. In the current sexual climate, sexual confusion has reached pandemic proportions. This is an explosive subject for another book. One's sexual orientation is one's own business and there is no judgment. However, let us be real about male, female, and other. If you are born male, whether you choose to cut off your private parts and repurpose them into the shape of a vulva will never make you a woman. You will be a transitioned male. The same goes for women who take hormones and have-a-penis-sewn-on, they will never be men, they will be a transitioned woman.

I am, in reality, presenting as a white, middle-aged woman with blonde hair and a mixed heritage. Should I decide to identify as a black male, does that make me a black man? If I take hormones and have bits of my body mutilated to give the impression of a black male, does that make me a black male? NO. Am I a pronoun? NO. Am I a cat? NO. End of story.

The confusion is the lack of comprehension of who we are as energetic, Spiritual Human beings.

Whilst wading through social media to wind down, I came across a meme that made me chuckle. It was a picture of Adam and Eve but the apple that Adam was eating was the hypodermis, not fruit from an apple tree. Apply all the information regarding the pineal and pituitary being reflected in the lower body and it might begin to make some sense. At the very least, it might amuse.

The Book of Enoch 24.1 - 25.7

24.1 And from there, I went to another place of the Earth, and he showed me a mountain of fire, that blazed day and night. 24.2 And I went towards it and saw seven magnificent mountains. And all were different from one another, and precious and beautiful stones, and all were precious, and their appearance glorious, and their form was beautiful. Three towards the east, one fixed firmly on another, and three towards the south, one on another, and deep and rugged valleys, no one of which was near another. 24.3 And there was a seventh mountain, in the middle of these, and in their height they were all like the seat of a throne; and fragrant trees surrounded it. 24.4 And there was, among them, a tree, such as I have never smelt, and none of them, nor any others, were like it. It smells more fragrant than any fragrance, and its leaves, and its flowers, and its wood never wither. Its fruit is good, and its fruit is like bunches of dates on a palm.24.5 And then I said: "Behold, this beautiful tree! Beautiful to look at, and pleasant are its leaves, and its fruit very delightful in appearance." 24.6 And then Michael, one of the Holy and Honoured Angels, who was with me, and was in charge of them, 25.1 answered me and said to me: "Enoch, why do you ask me about the fragrance of this tree, and why do you inquire to learn?"25.2 Then I, Enoch, answered him saying: "I wish to learn about everything, but especially about this tree." 25.3 And he answered me, saying: "This high mountain, which you saw, whose summit is like the Throne of the Lord, is the throne where the Holy and Great One, the Lord of Glory, the Eternal King, will sit when He comes down to visit the Earth for good. 25.4 And this beautiful fragrant tree, and no creature of flesh has authority to touch it until the Great Judgement, when He will take vengeance on all, and bring everything to a consummation forever; this will be given to the righteous and the humble. 25.5 From its fruit, life will be given to the chosen; towards the north it will be planted, in a Holy place, by the house of the Lord, the Eternal King. 25.6 .... They will each draw the fragrance of it into their bones, and they will live a long life on Earth, as your fathers lived. And, in their days, sorrow and pain, and toil and punishment, will not touch them."

The book of Enoch is describing the same thing as the Bible. The inner mind and the outer expression of it.

The seven mountains are the seven energy centres of the body, etc., etc.

The question remains of who wrote the biblical scripts? Who re-edited them? Who changed their original meaning? Who took the sacred books out? Who would turn a beautiful creation into a demonised, mental weapon to create fear and control over innocent people and why? Who would take the beautiful, metaphorical language and use it for selfish gain, claiming it for themselves? Who would take all the real knowledge out of it and hide the truth? Who, indeed, would call themselves the elite or chosen ones, leaving the rest of the world indoctrinated and enslaved at their feet? I wonder? Who and what would be so divisive?

In my opinion, some of the biblical scripts are prophetic, spirit breathed, and authentically ancient. Some, however, are derived, or perhaps one could say stolen, from even more ancient and great civilisations that go back to previous eras on this planet. For example, the Egyptian Books of Thoth and Set, the incredible intelligence issuing from Kush and African civilisations who invented incredible technologies that are still occluded from us today. Now who and why would Kush be destroyed? Why would the black races become enslaved, oppressed, and whitewashed — and what the hell for?

In my own life, I present as blonde and blue eyed. However, go back two generations and my Great Grandmother looks very North

African indeed. My daughter is half African and my life has been a white water ride in terms of prejudice and liberation. Excuse the pun.

I have a birthmark which is the Egyptian symbol for Isis or the third eye on my right finger. I am left-handed and have a very rare blood group. My resonance freaks most people out and I have been either totally rejected or totally loved with nothing in between all my life. My battle has been long and I sometimes grow weary.

You see, the real truth is that everything, the true Law of God, the innerverse, and everything is written into our DNA. All we need do is activate it. At this point in time, on this particular timeline, there is a movement toward changing the human DNA through injection and other sly means. A clandestine operation, a lockstep production that would have us marching to a very, very dissonant tune. "They" have created their own Satan, their own devils, which they try to inflict upon us. Thankfully, they will be killed by them, themselves and good riddance.

I recently noticed the similarities between Kemetic philosophy, Judaism, and Christianity.

KEMETIC is similar to the word HERMETIC and we know from Gerald Massey's research that the Judea-Christian religion has Kemetic origins.

"A brief explanation is in order. African civilizations ranging from Kemet / Egypt in North Africa to Chou Civilization in Southern Asia (the area now called China) were invaded by Aryan predators (now called Europeans, Arabs, and Asians) beginning approximately 1,500 BCE (Before Common Era). With each civilization / society that was conquered the invaders used the spoils to fabricate societies of their own; the invaders of China created Jainism and Confucianism; those in India created Brahmanism; those in Asia Minor created Zoroastrianism, and Judaism; and those invading Kemet created "Greek Philosophy", Christianity and Islam.

"As a part of the process of domination each invading group claimed authorship of the knowledge base and technology they appropriated from their victims. Each one claimed what they fabricated to have no relationship whatsoever with the civilization / society of the invaded population. Christianity is espoused in this fashion." (Ref: 133 and 134)

Ultimately, it's about time that we all realised that we are one. One being. One collective. We all have the same truth written inside our DNA on every level of our beings and we are all individual expressions of the Divine — regardless of the apparent external differences.

We all need to apologise to each other for all we have done in our ignorance and for our ancestors' mistakes. No one is without fault. Being a human is to forgive each other's lack, not continue with separation and hatred. We are better than that! Aren't we?

Divine, infinite truth resides within the hearts and minds of every living being whether they know it or not. If you call it the Christ, so be it. If you call it enlightenment, nirvana, awakened, Sun worshipper, whatever you name it, ultimately, the key to unlock the truth is love. That's what we are all learning about, regardless of who you are, pauper or elite.

Where did the knowledge of God come from in the first place?

We need to forgive everyone for everything in all dimensions of time and space, unconditionally, and set them free from bondage. That doesn't mean we agree with their transgressions, it means we are liberating each other from the weight of sin and turning that vibration off.

We are all Africans.

We are all Greeks, Chinese, 'Originee, and Inuit.

We are all part of each other and need to uphold each other's dignity and self-belief, starting with ourselves and our children.

NB: Note the origin of the word Nephilim: (Ref: 135) *Niflheim, Old Norse Niflheimr, in Norse mythology, the cold, dark, misty world of the dead, ruled by the goddess Hel. In some accounts it was the last of nine worlds, a place into which evil men passed after reaching the region of death (Hel). Situated below one of the roots of the world tree, Yggdrasill, Niflheim contained a well, Hvergelmir, from which many rivers flowed. In the Norse creation story, Niflheim was the misty region north of the void (Ginnungagap) in which the world was created.

"Not only do they hold up the sky, but more than any other living things, trees define our sense of place and provide much needed equilibrium" (Ref 136: Earnhardt. T. 'Trees hold up the sky')

We are beautiful trees. Walking, talking, living trees, breathing in air and sunlight, photosynthesising thoughts and intentions, vibrating with every living creature on this plane.

Just like trees, we blossom and give of ourselves so others may live. Our fruit may be seen or unseen but our mere existence is miraculous. I believe that this is a time where we shall be reconciled unto ourselves and as a collective consciousness, ascend to a greater awareness of our true nature. We have a lot to learn from our magnificent trees, whose roots hold the soil together and whose leaves mirror the stars.

Chapter 11
Awakened Trees

AS WE COME TO OUR OWN unique comprehension of who we are, who and what God is in relation to ourselves and each other, and as this, our incredible truth, penetrates the current global deception, obliterating the old, worn-out lies that have kept humanity voluntarily enslaved for thousands of years, there is a new dawn on the horizon; a new yet ancient song calling to us from within our own hearts. There's a yearning and an ache for the end of pain, sorrow, despair, war, deception, ignorance, racism, murder, pedophilia, stupidity, and hate.

There is a glorious, awakened place beyond culture, beyond differences, beyond reactive minds, where we can meet each other and know that it's through grace we have been born, have lived, and experienced this moment in time. As we travel through our inner and outer worlds, we now have the opportunity to be our own masters and empower others to be the same in their own lives.

There's no judgement of wrongs because if there were then we would all be burning and adding fuel to the fire. There isn't one being on this plane that is perfect. Not one. So therefore, not one of us can judge another for anything they may have done, no matter how vile or disrespectful.

It's my hope that inner wisdom and truth is activated within each and every one of us so strongly that we cause a tidal wave of revelation. The Book of Revelation is our walk toward the infinite, not emblematic of war and external destruction. However, if these lower vibrations insist on taking things literally and creating havoc, then they will have to pick up the pieces themselves as they wander through the wreckage, subjects of their own demonic laws, dead by their own hands.

It is time to change the script(ures).

It is time to make a decision not to fulfil the book and in fact, create in alignment with God. It is not time to kill everything and everyone and build back better — that's not going to work. It's time to reveal the simple truths about life, history, our minds, bodies, souls, and spirits.

In this book, I have given a just few examples of how the external symbols, myths, and stories are telling us that everything we seek is inside of us, from the Garden of Eden inside our head to the biomagnetic field that stores excess memory and energy.

I have hoped to inspire you to go and research more about your brain and its capacity. I've hoped to strip away a little of the old mind-programming, demonisation, and superstition so you can live freely — without guilt and dishonour.

I have hoped that the old patterns of thinking may have been challenged and perhaps even inspired new thoughts. In a way, I could keep on writing forever, but that is not the purpose of this book. This is a quantum doorway (for those who have the eyes to see it) that leads to a clearer view of the marvellous creation that surrounds us.

Our quantum abilities to be conscious in more than one timeline at once can be activated through a simple realisation that we are the master of our timelines and centre of our wheel.

As we reach, we will be met. The deeper we go, the more Divine love there is to uphold us.

The process of awakening can be harsh, especially if we hold on too tightly to what needs to go, but, if we let go and trust, the invisible becomes visible and makes itself known to us. We just need a little faith.

As I sit here, exhausted by the process of completing this cycle, I am grateful and expanded by all I have learned. I know I have not even scratched the surface.

We have the power to change this timeline but we all need to do it together, without the need to control others or exercise our own egos. If we play to our strengths and empower each other to be our best selves, we will make it through. Let us do it for our kids and the animals we love so dearly.

We don't need anything or anybody to tell us how to be if we tune into the inner voice.

To conclude:

"You can not enslave a man and say that he's a human being, that he has humanity and that he was one of the forerunners of the world's religion. You can not enslave an African and say this about him, because if you say he's a human being, then you're saying he's an extension of you... then you can not sell an African Christianity and call him a heathen and acknowledge the African contribution towards the creation of Christianity..." ref: Prof. John Henrick Clarke 1973 interview

This is just the beginning of the lifting of the veil, the Arachnoid Mater.

Now we know that the ark of our covenant in the centre of our heads, our Garden of Eden and Tree of life, I postulate the beginning of the golden age has indeed arrived and through the power of our own divine connection and oneness in spirit, as the Hopis say: "We are the people we have been waiting for."

End Notes:

Bibliography / References / Images

Chapter One

1.https://pubmed.ncbi.nlm.nih.gov/ 1305634/[1]

2.https://www.sciencedirect.com/topics/biochemistry-genetics-and-molecular-biology/pineal-gland-function

3. Hongzhi. Li " Zhuan Falun"

4. Prof. Lili Feng and et al

5.http://www.sadhsangat.com/dasam-duar-the-tenth-gate-revised/

6.Steve Lecaz. Engineer. https://www.linkedin.com/in/stevelecaz/

7.http://www.flameinmind.com/outervision/.

8.5G Research: https://5g-emf.com/5g-the-pineal-gland-aluminium-glyphosate-fluoride-wi-fi/

CHAPTER TWO

9.VIDEO 'IT'S TIME to wake up the trees' https://bit.ly/timetowakeupthetrees

10. Pineal info: https://pubmed.ncbi.nlm.nih.gov/8788489/

11. Jenny. H., "Cymatics. A Study of Wave Phenomena and Vibration"

12. All 11 Dimensions: www.yourtube.com/watch?v=UxubeeSqSmk[2]

13. Clean Slate / Root Brand: https://therootbrands.com/freebeing1966

---

1. https://pubmed.ncbi.nlm.nih.gov/%25252525201305634/

2. http://www.yourtube.com/watch?v=UxubeeSqSmk

14. Dana Zohar "The Quantum Self".

15.Moontracks: https://www.moontracks.com/moon2023.html?Month=1

16.   Daily   Chakra   Meditation: https://drive.google.com/file/d/1afow_zGC8GxHQ3PWxc3vJXfm1P-l9IGJ/view?usp=share_link

Chapter 3

———————

17. GALATIANS 2:20 (Bible) "I have been crucified with Christ and it is no longer I who live, but Christ lives in me and the life which I now live in the flesh, I live by faith in the Son (sun) of God, who loved me and gave himself up for me"

18. www.sabbathcovenant.com[3]

19. Over-toning with Anna-Maria Hefele www.youtube.com/watch?v=vC9Qh709gas&t=13s[4]

20. https://www.abarim-publications.com/Meaning/Ephesus.html

21. Bernstein on The Harmonic Series www.youtube.com/watch?v=9HjEAtJXssc[5]

22.Dream dictionary https://www.auntyflo.com/dream-dictionary/fish-symbol-meaning

23. The legend of the Nommos https://www.bibliotecapleyades.net/esp_dogon04.htm https://www.bibliotecapleyades.net/esp_dogon04.htm

24. Temple. R "The Sirius Mystery

24.1 Kali and the Rectum: https://youtu.be/cj1c7dp0zV0

25. Alterovitz.G The Harvard Crimson: https://www.thecrimson.com/article/2007/4/26/tf-translates-dna-into-music-sequence/

26. Tonya Cannariato (Author/Editor)

27. It's time to wake up the trees part two: www.youtube.com/watch?v=cj1c7dp0zV0[6]

---

3. http://18.www.sabbathcovenant.com/

4. http://www.youtube.com/watch?v=vC9Qh709gas&t=13s

5. http://www.youtube.com/watch?v=9HjEAtJXssc

6. http://www.youtube.com/watch?v=cj1c7dp0zV0

28.   Myrrh: http://www.efloras.org/florataxon.aspx?flora_id=5&taxon_id=107780

29   https://judaism.stackexchange.com/questions/65726/does-the-talmud-promote-pedophilia

30.Raising the Chrism: https://archive.org/details/the-sacred-secret-of-the-christ-within-raising-the-chrism

31.Definitions https://www.abarim-publications.com/Meaning/John.html

31.1 Professor Alan Rice:

"Alan Rice, DESc, received his degree from Columbia University and has had a diverse career. He was a professor of geophysics, geology, sustainability, oceanography, physics and engineering at various institutes: Woods Hole Oceanographic Institution, University of Chicago, University of Pretoria (South Africa), University of Utrecht (The Netherlands), The University of Newcastle upon Tyne (England), etc.. Rice made significant contributions to the advancement of green practices and developed geographic information systems (GIS) for National Parks, including the development of game parks in South Africa. He has worked on issues relating to nuclear physics and engineering, e.g., power supplies and radioactive waste disposal. Rice was Chief Scientist on oceanographic vessels and was also involved with deep submersibles. He served as Director of the Consortium for Computational Fluid Dynamics Modeling (CFD) of Ore Body Formation. While working at Stony Brook University, Southampton, NY, and in the division of Earth and Planetary Sciences at the American Museum of Natural History, he conducted research on the occurrence and consequences of multiple meteoritic impacts in Antarctica. He frequently collaborated with the Hayden Planetarium. He has been an Advisory Board member of Hamptons Observatory since its inception." (https://www.hamptonsobservatory.org/alan-rice-bio.

32. The Lotus Effect: https://www.teachengineering.org/lessons/view/duk_surfacetensionunit_less4)

33. Derivation of Temple: https://www.etymonline.com/word/Temple

34. Derivation of Church https://www.etymonline.com/search?q=church&type=5

35. Hittite Etymological Dictionary. Puhvel.J : https://www.scribd.com/document/414470855/Jaan-Puhvel-Hittite-Etymological-Dictionary-Vol-bookos-z1-org-pdf

36. Revelation 3.14 "This is the message from the one who is the Amen—the faithful and true witness, the beginning of God's new creation.."

37.Revelation 2:9 'I know about the slander of those who say they are Jews and are not, but are a synagogue of Satan...'

38. Revelation 2:10 'Don't be afraid of what you are about to suffer. The devil will throw some of you into prison to test you. You will suffer for ten days. But if you remain faithful even when facing death, I will give you the crown of life.'

39.The new definition of woman: https://dictionary.cambridge.org/dictionary/english/woman

40. Solar Plexus - Websters English Dictionary: https://www.merriam-webster.com/dictionary/solar%20plexus[7]

40.1 (To do) Black box, cross, tesseract, solar plexus, shiva and the language of the body see video reference: https://bit.ly/referencetesseract

41. Bible: Luke 8:11 The seed is the word. Adapted by 2 songwriters "and the word is the beginning". Please see video: 'Sublime Time' on www.andromedalighpress.com

42. Oneness/Esho Funi: http://tibetanbuddhistencyclopedia.com/en/index.php?title=Oneness_of_life_and_its_environment

43.Origin, 3rd century CE Egyptian, Christian theologian Origen (184–253 CE), an ancient Greek scholar and ascetic.

44. Bill Donahue Sol-ohm-on : www.youtube.com/watch?v=UFrUpr5-bmE&t=33s[8]

---

7. https://www.merriam-webster.com/dictionary/solar%25252520plexus

8. http://www.youtube.com/watch?v=UFrUpr5-bmE&t=33s

45. The testament of King Solomon: http://esotericarchives.com/solomon/testamen.htm

46.Sardis: https://en.wikipedia.org/wiki/Chalcedony)

47. Bible, Revelation 3:1.

48.Britannica, The Editors of Encyclopaedia. "chalcedony". Encyclopedia Britannica, 24 Jan. 2020, https://www.britannica.com/science/chalcedony.

49. Hormones crystalline structure: https://www.sciencedirect.com/science/article/pii/B9780125711340500168

50.Proverbs 18:21 Bible

51.Bible, Revelation 3:7-13

52.'Philo' The Free Dictionary: https://www.thefreedictionary.com/philo-

53. Britannica, The Editors of Encyclopaedia. "Attalus II Philadelphus ("Brotherly")". Encyclopedia Britannica, 17 Apr. 2020, https://www.britannica.com/biography/Attalus-II-Philadelphus.

54. Adelphi definition: https://www.etymonline.com/word/adelphi

55. Delphi/Dolphin in the brain: www.youtube.com/watch?v=EhT1r9uOzT0[9]

56.Definition of Dolphin: https://www.etymonline.com/word/dolphin?ref=etymonline_crossreference

57. Dorado constellation lies in the southern hemisphere. Its name means "the dolphinfish" (Coryphaena hippurus) in Spanish. The constellation has also been depicted as a swordfish. https://www.constellation-guide.com/constellation-list/dorado-constellation/

58.Dolphinfish live: https://theskylive.com/sky/constellations/dorado-constellation

59.Bible:Revelation 3:7

60.Hans Jenny Cymatics: https://geometrymatters.com/hans-jenny-and-the-science-of-sound-cymatics/

61. Bible, Revelation 3:8

62. Krishnamurti: https://libquotes.com/jiddu-krishnamurti/quotes/love

63. Bible: Revelation 3:14-22

66.Hippocampus definition: https://www.merriam-webster.com/dictionary/hippocampus

64.https://jnnp.bmj.com/content/71/3/351)

65.Image: www.youtube.com/watch?v=veEoelSWDCs[10]

66.www.findyourvoiceandroar.com[11]

67. The Limbic system: https://www.thoughtco.com/limbic-system-anatomy-373200

68. Matthew 14:35-36 New King James Version : **35** And when the men of that place recognized Him, they sent out into all that surrounding region, brought to Him all who were sick, **36** and begged Him that they might only touch the hem of His garment. And as many as touched *it* were made perfectly well.

CHAPTER 4

69.LIMBIC SYSTEM: https://www.verywellhealth.com/the-limbic-system-2488579

70.Ouroborus: https://www.britannica.com/topic/Ouroboros

71. https://jnnp.bmj.com/content/71/3/351

---

10. http://www.youtube.com/watch?v=veEoelSWDCs

11. http://66.www.findyourvoiceandroar.com/

72. https://torah.org/rosh-hashanah/shofar/

73. Bible: https://www.biblehub.com/matthew/7-7.htm

74. Bible: https://biblehub.com/context/revelation/19-11.htm

75.The Hippocampus, Ouroborous, Pegasus, White horse, Sea Horse, Ram's Horn, Ammonite and Horn of Plenty.

76.Ark of the covenant https://biblehub.com/1_kings/6-27.htm

77.Hippocampus anatomy https://anatomyinfo.com/hippocampus-anatomy/

78.Amygdala: https://www.verywellhealth.com/amygdala-5112775#:~:text=The%20amygdalae%20interpret%20external%20stim[12]).

79.Ezekiel Bible: https://www.biblegateway.com/passage/?search=ezekiel%2041&version=NKJV[13]

80. Foramen: https://biologydictionary.net/foramen/)

81.Holy Spirit: https://www.biblegateway.com/passage/?search=John%2014:26&version=NKJV[14]

82. https://bit.ly/reference82pyramidinhead

83.The Veil https://bible-history.com/tabernacle/the-veil

84.Delta fornicis https://medical-dictionary.thefreedictionary.com/delta+fornicis

---

CHAPTER 5

12. https://www.verywellhealth.com/amygdala-5112775%2523:~:text=The%25252520amygdalae%25252520interpret%25252520external%25252520stimuli,%25252525Dor%25252525Dfight%25252520response

13. https://www.biblegateway.com/passage/?search=ezekiel%2525252041&version=NKJV

14. https://www.biblegateway.com/passage/?search=John%2525252014:26&version=NKJV

85.   Fornax   constellation:https://theskylive.com/sky/constellations/fornax-constellation

86. Bible: 1 John 1:5 "This is the message we have heard from him and declare to you: God is light; in him there is no darkness at all."

87.Light waves https://wonders.physics.wisc.edu/what-is-light/

88.Bible: Genesis 1:27 "So God created man in His *own* image; in the image of God He created him; male and female He created them."

89.   https://earthsky.org/space/largest-oldest-mass-of-water-in-universe-discovered/)

90.Medical   dictionary   -   https://medical-dictionary.thefreedictionary.com/commissura+fornicis

91. Sonic waves https://en.wikipedia.org/wiki/Faraday_wave

92. The shape of sound www.youtube.com/LTlpGd1qN28/edit[15]

CHAPTER 6

93. Star facts: https://www.star-facts.com/alnitak/

94.The letter Z https://en.wikipedia.org/wiki/Z_(military_symbol)

95.Resistor   https://www.techtarget.com/whatis/definition/resistor#:~:text=A%20resistor%20is%20an%20electrical,device%20such%20as%20a%2[0] [16]

96.Ohm's law https://www.linquip.com/blog/resistance-vs-impedance/

------

15. http://www.youtube.com/LTlpGd1qN28/edit

16. https://www.techtarget.com/whatis/definition/
    resistor%252523:~:text=A%25252520resistor%25252520is%25252520an%25252520electrical,device%25
    252520such%25252520as%25252520a%25252520transistor

97.BIBLE 1 KINGS 8:1 "Now Solomon assembled the elders of Israel and all the heads of the tribes, the chief fathers of the children of Israel, to King Solomon in Jerusalem, that they might bring up the ark of the covenant of the Lord from the City of David, which *is* Zion."

98.Bible 1 Kings 9 https://www.biblegateway.com/passage/?search=1+Kings+9&version=NKJV

CHAPTER 7

99.WWW.YOUTUBE.COM/SCKOTGJNTRK/edit[17]

100. Sound changes the DNA https://www.mindlab.institute/blog/scientists-prove-dna-can-be-reprogrammed-by-our-own-words

101. Find your voice and roar www.findyourvoiceandroar.com[18]

102. Medical News. https://www.medicalnewstoday.com/articles/321037

103. Genesis 4:1-18

104. Cain and Abel Quran 5:27-31[19]:

105. Video: https://bit.ly/explanation-Hypo-hippo + images: https://bit.ly/Mammilliary-images

106. Sound changes the DNA: https://www.mindlab.institute/blog/scientists-prove-dna-can-be-reprogrammed-by-our-own-words

107. The shape of sound: https://bit.ly/the-shape-of-sound

108. See reference 105

109. The Psalterium and Lira: https://bit.ly/psalterium-ref109

---

17. http://99.www.youtube.com/sckOtgJNtrk/edit

18. http://www.findyourvoiceandroar.com/

19. https://en.wikipedia.org/wiki/Quran_5:27-31

110. Bible: 1 Samuel Chapter 16 https://www.biblegateway.com/passage/?search=1%20Samuel%2016&version=KJV[20]

111. Arc of the Covenant / Mercy Seat/ Sphenoid bone:

https://bit.ly/sphenoid-arc-of-covenant111

———————————

112.BIBLE EZEKIEL 25:10-22

25 The word of the Lord came to me: **2** "Son of man, set your face against the **Ammonites** and prophesy against them. **3** Say to them, 'Hear the word of the Sovereign Lord. This is what the Sovereign Lord says: Because you said "Aha!" over my sanctuary when it was desecrated and over the land of Israel when it was laid waste and over the people of Judah when they went into exile, **4** therefore I am going to give you to the people of the East as a possession. They will set up their camps and pitch their tents among you; they will eat your fruit and drink your milk. **5** I will turn Rabbah into a pasture for camels and Ammon into a resting place for sheep. Then you will know that I am the Lord. **6** For this is what the Sovereign Lord says: Because you have clapped your hands and stamped your feet, rejoicing with all the malice of your heart against the land of Israel, **7** therefore I will stretch out my hand against you and give you as plunder to the nations. I will wipe you out from among the nations and exterminate you from the countries. I will destroy you, and you will know that I am the Lord.'"

———————————

113. CRISTA GALI CRIBIFORM Plate: www.youtube.com/watch?v=mz6sas4jVMc[21]

114. 12 Cranial Nerves + images: https://bit.ly/reference114-24-elders

———————————

CHAPTER 8

20. https://www.biblegateway.com/passage/?search=1%25252520Samuel%2525252016&version=KJV

21. http://www.youtube.com/watch?v=mz6sas4jVMc

115. Bible: 1 Corinthinans 13: https://www.biblegateway.com/passage/?search=1%20Corinthians%2013&version=NIV[22]

116. Baphomet: https://bit.ly/levi-image-bapho

117. Atbash Cipher: https://www.boxentriq.com/code-breaking/atbash-cipher

118. Alterovitz.G. (2007) The Crimson: https://www.thecrimson.com/article/2007/4/26/tf-translates-dna-into-music-sequence/)

---

119. BIBLE: GENESIS 1:26 https://www.biblegateway.com/passage/?search=Genesis+1%3A26&version=NIV[23]

---

120. TEDDY AND THURSDAY: https://bit.ly/tedandthursaudio121. Encyclopedia Britannica https://www.britannica.com/topic/Yggdrasill

122.Tom Earnhardt. Wrap News. https://legacy.wral.com/coronavirus/tom-earnhardt-trees-hold-up-the-sky/19375705/

123. Encyclopedia Britannica 124. https://www.reference.com/science/function-arbor-vitae-c519f4e32133f7dd

125. https://mudfooted.com/the-arbor-vitae-the-tree-of-life/

CHAPTER 9

---

126. GANESH BACK OF THE brain: please go to Ref 114 at 1 min and 38 seconds

---

22. https://www.biblegateway.com/passage/?search=1%25252520Corinthians%2525252013&version=NIV

23. https://www.biblegateway.com/passage/?search=Genesis+1%2525253A26&version=NIV

127. Trees and mycelium - https://www.theguardian.com/commentisfree/2020/oct/10/hidden-world-fungi-life-earth and Merlin Sheldrake: https://www.merlinsheldrake.com/articles

128. Indian Gods: please rewatch reference 114 with the knowledge that each Indian and Judeo- Christian God represents a part of our physiology

129. Images of brain: For a detailed three-dimensional view of the brain and all I have been speaking about, I suggest you download the Complete Anatomy App. https://bit.ly/anatomyappcomplete

---

CHAPTER 10

130. Set https://kentakepage.com/the-10-virtues-of-the-kemetic-ancient-egyptian-mystery-teachings/

131.3rd Ventricle: https://teachmeanatomy.info/neuroanatomy/vessels/ventricles/

132. Arachnoid Mater: 'Animal Speak' page 344 (Andrews.T.)

133. Kemetic:)https://www.africanamerica.org/topic/kemetic-egyptian-origin-of-christianity[24])

133. Crusades: https://www.history.com/topics/middle-ages/crusades

134 /135. Nephilim: Bible – Genesis 6:2 https://www.biblegateway.com/verse/en/Genesis%206:2 [25]and

Enoch 1:6-8 https://readingacts.com/2016/05/31/the-fallen-angels-1-enoch-6-8/

136. Tom Earnhardt. Wrap News: https://legacy.wral.com/coronavirus/tom-earnhardt-trees-hold-up-the-sky/19375705/

---

24. https://www.africanamerica.org/topic/kemetic-egyptian-origin-of-christianity
25. https://www.biblegateway.com/verse/en/Genesis%252525206:2

CHAPTER 11

HTTPS://EN.WIKIPEDIA.org/wiki/Boustrophedon[26]

---

26. https://en.wikipedia.org/wiki/Boustrophedon

About the Author

Andromeda Lightfoot is a spiritual warrior, a mother, musician, published singer-songwriter and researcher. Her journey has been one of deep personal transformation which is reflected in all her works and has brought her to a place of insight and depth for such a time as this.

Read more at andromedalightpress.com.

Ingram Content Group UK Ltd.
Milton Keynes UK
UKHW020624110523
421574UK00013B/428

9 798215 204511